Write Like
Lee Child

A study guide focusing on
the novel Killing Floor

MATTHEW MCGUINNESS

SPECIAL OFFER

A comprehensive set of exercises accompanies *Write Like Lee Child*. The 35-page workbook will walk you through the process of planning a novel in the style of Lee Child, and help you practise thriller-writing techniques.

To receive the writing exercises for FREE, all you have to do is sign up for my *Popular Fiction Masterclass* email newsletter. Turn to the back of the book now to find out how you can do that.

ABOUT THE SERIES

Popular Fiction Masterclass is a series of study guides designed to help writers learn from bestselling authors. Each book focuses on a single bestselling novel, explaining what makes it great and how to emulate it. To find out more, go to the following Web address.

http://popularfictionmasterclass.com/about/

ABOUT THE AUTHOR

Matthew McGuinness is a graduate of the prestigious Creative Writing MA at the University of East Anglia. He blogs on the subject of writerly craft and works as an editor and copywriter.

CONTENTS

INTRODUCTION

It has always puzzled me that writers aren't encouraged to learn by consciously studying the masters. Think about how painters and sculptors have traditionally learned their art. Until the early twentieth century, they'd study the work of great artists from the ancient world. The idea was to learn every gesture and nuance used by the ancient Greeks. And when you fully understood the craft and sentiment behind those great works of the past, you could begin creating your own original pieces, but always in a way that owed something to the spirit of the Greeks.

In my opinion, writers should learn their art in exactly the same way. That's why I started writing my series of *Popular Fiction Masterclass* books. Think of each one as a period of study in front of an Old Master painting – a preparation for creating original work, inspired by a great example. And there can be few examples better than Lee Child. He wrote his first novel, *Killing Floor*, in 1993 after losing his job in television, and it was an almost overnight success. The author claims that, amazingly, he hadn't written one word of prose fiction before starting it! Few of us can lay claim to talent of that calibre, but by taking the time to understand what it is that makes *Killing Floor* so great, it's possible to grow as a writer.

Like all of my *Popular Fiction Masterclass* study guides, this book begins with a full summary of the novel under consideration. After that, the chapters are arranged thematically. They provide in-depth analyses of nine different aspects Lee Child's writing, and end with a handy summary of key points.

Here are the areas that I'll be covering.

- What makes for an appealing main character in a thriller novel?
- Is thriller fiction all about 'good guys' and 'bad guys'?
- How do you create a cast of characters with maximum dramatic potential?
- What are the structures that underlie a good story? Which creative-writing experts should you trust?
- How do you create a mystery that keeps readers turning the pages?
- What will ensure that the reader has a satisfying emotional experience through your novel?
- How do you connect with the reader's beliefs and aspirations to convey a message?
- What are the essential skills in the toolkit of a great storyteller?

But that's not all. If you sign up for my email list, you can also get access to a free set of exercises. These challenging and varied activities will help you put into practice the many lessons that you've learned from *Killing Floor*. They provide days, if not weeks of targeted writing practice and novel-planning activities. If you work through them all in a committed way, you will have gained valuable experience of a practical creative process, but, more importantly, you'll have a whole load of material that will feed directly into your novel. If that sounds good, go to the special offer page at the end of this book and find out how to get hold of the exercises.

SUMMARY OF KILLING FLOOR

Chapter 1

- The unidentified first-person narrator is sitting in a diner, eating.
- He's arrested by police in a highly professional operation. They treat him as a major threat.
- He's taken by car to the police headquarters at Margrave, a small town in Georgia.

Chapter 2

- The narrator is processed by the police – fingerprints taken, etc.
- We are introduced to several police characters: the brutal Chief Morrison, the professional Detective Finlay and the kind, attractive Detective Roscoe.
- During the ensuing interview, we finally learn the narrator's name: Jack Reacher.
- We also learn that Reacher is a wanderer.
- His reason for being in town is to pay homage to Blind Blake, a blues singer.
- Finlay asks if Reacher knows the meaning of the word 'pluribus'.
- Finally, we hear the details of the crime he's accused of. It's murder.

- A piece of paper has been found on the dead body. It bears the word 'pluribus' and a telephone number.
- We receive a physical description of Reacher as the crime is described. He's a big guy.
- We learn that he was a military policeman.
- Reacher must wait in a cell while his background is checked.
- The interview resumes. Chief Morrison himself emerges as a witness, claiming that he saw Reacher near the crime scene.

Chapter 3

- Reacher reveals his investigative abilities. With great psychological insight into the ways of killers, he argues that there must have been a team of three.
- Reacher tries to help the cops exonerate him before a bus arrives to take him to prison for the weekend.
- On calling the telephone number on the piece of paper, they discover that it belongs to Paul Hubble, a local banker.

Chapter 4

- Reacher flirts with Roscoe the female cop.
- Paul Hubble is brought into the police headquarters. He's a yuppie.
- Hubble confesses to the killing and is placed in the cell with Reacher.
- There's an alibi he chose not to exploit: a policeman was with Hubble at the time of the murder.
- Neither Reacher nor Finlay can understand why Hubble confessed if he obviously wasn't the killer.

Chapter 5

- Reacher and Hubble go off on the bus to prison.
- The two of them are placed in a cell and bed down for the night.

Chapter 6

- In the morning, Reacher speaks with an old prisoner and works out that they've been placed with dangerous lifers.
- A gang of prisoners tries to persecute Hubble, but Reacher gets rid of them.
- Reacher asks Hubble why he confessed for no reason, but gets no answer.
- Hubble gives a bit more information. Someone is threatening him with violence.

Chapter 7

- Reacher and Hubble continue their discussion.
- We hear that a previous head detective killed himself.
- Hubble talks about how the word 'pluribus' surprised him in the police interview. He refuses to say why.
- The Aryan Brotherhood attack Reacher in the prison bathroom.
- Reacher and Hubble are rescued by Spivey, the prison warder, and taken to the remand floor, where they should have been all along.
- Reacher realises that he was set up for the attack by Spivey.

Chapter 8

- Hubble opens up about the plot a bit more and says there are ten people involved and their scheme remains vulnerable until a key event takes place on Sunday. He will not say any more than that.
- Reacher talks about his past and the experience of leaving the military as it down-sized after the Cold War.
- Reacher guesses that Hubble confessed because he wanted to be safe in prison.
- After leaving the prison, Reacher is picked up by Roscoe. Hubble is picked up by his wife.
- According to Roscoe, Reacher has been exonerated.
- Reacher notices a suspicious occurrence: his own fingerprints took a long time to get identified, whereas those of the murdered man did not.

- Reacher offers to buy Roscoe lunch and she accepts.

Chapter 9

- Reacher goes to pick up his stuff from the police headquarters before heading into town.
- Reacher remarks on the tidiness of the place.
- A woman drinking coffee in the same convenience store as Reacher seems to be in distress.
- She is picked up by her stepson in a black pickup.
- The store owner explains that the woman's family, the Kliners, are important local business people. They own the warehouse where the murder occurred.
- Reacher goes to the barber. The old guy working there is not keen to talk about the Kliners.
- The barber does confirm that someone killed Blind Blake, as Reacher had heard.
- Back at the police headquarters, Reacher is told that a new body has been found.
- The victim has been identified as someone called 'Sherman'.
- Joining in with the investigation, Reacher heads over to the mortuary with Finlay and Roscoe.
- In the course of the discussion, Reacher realises that the first murder victim was his brother.

Chapter 10

- Reacher tries to understand why his brother Joe was in Margrave. It would be too much of a coincidence if it were not connected with the conspiracy described by Hubble.
- Reacher commits himself to taking revenge on his brother's killers and finishing Joe's mission, whatever it was.
- He's interviewed by Finlay about his brother's murder and warned not to take matters into his own hands.
- Reacher goes with Roscoe to get some answers from Hubble.
- Hubble's wife Charlie is there but not Hubble himself.

- Reacher and Roscoe have sex.
- Hubble still can't be contacted.
- Reacher meets Roscoe in the diner where he was arrested.
- The son of Kliner, the local businessman, is offended by Reacher and Roscoe's affection for one another.
- Roscoe explains that the second body was identified as Sherman Stoller from fingerprints.
- Roscoe is called away and Reacher guesses that it's because Hubble is dead.

Chapter 11

- Reacher starts to piece together a story that explains his misadventures over the last couple of days. He believes Hubble was the target in prison, and that, because Reacher was wearing glasses and Hubble had lost his, the Aryan Brotherhood went for the wrong man.
- The black pickup that came for the Kliner woman follows Reacher.
- Reacher goes to the Hubble house, feeling guilty that he apparently got his cellmate killed.
- He encounters Hubble's wife, Charlie, who doesn't look like a woman whose husband has been murdered.
- He goes to find Roscoe at the police headquarters, still feeling ashamed that he got Hubble killed.
- Another murder has indeed occurred, but it turns out that it was not Hubble. It was the police chief and his wife.

Chapter 12

- Finlay expresses his disillusion with the town and its mayor, Teale, who is an old-school southern reactionary.
- They go to the convenience store for coffee, doughnuts and a talk. Finlay gives an unflattering account of his recruitment by the Margrave authorities.
- Leaving the convenience store, they visit the crime scene before returning to town.

Chapter 13

- Reacher and Finlay discuss the gory details of the crime as they walk into town and back to the police headquarters.
- Reacher starts to make links between Hubble's story told in prison and the latest murder.
- He continues to wonder about the reason for his brother's presence in Margrave. He was clearly investigating something.
- The mystery of Hubble's whereabouts is pondered too. Surely, he's dead.
- The black pickup is seen again. Kliner stares at Reacher.
- Reacher suggests that Finlay could be next in line for murder, given that the police chief was killed.
- They agree on their next investigative steps.
- An aggressive encounter between Reacher and Kliner's son takes place on the street. Kliner's son claims to have a romantic link with Roscoe.

Chapter 14

- Mayor Teale is at the police headquarters. He's taking over personal control of the police department and pushing forward their investigation into Morrison's death.
- Finlay and Reacher must now conspire behind Teale's back.
- They know from Hubble's prison ramblings that something important is happening on Sunday as part of the criminal conspiracy. They must find out what.
- They contact Picard, an FBI agent who has agreed to help Finlay.
- An apparently courteous exchange between Reacher and the mayor is actually full of mutual suspicion.
- He returns to the Hubble residence, spotting some Hispanic men who are acting suspiciously.
- At the Hubble house, Charlie engages him to find her husband. Reacher still thinks Hubble's dead, but agrees.
- He asks her about the word 'pluribus', which was written on the scrap of paper found on Joe's body. She can't help.

- Reacher tells Charlie to go to an FBI safe house with Picard.
- Picard, who is an enormous guy, arrives and takes Charlie to safety.

Chapter 15

- Reacher goes to confront Spivey, the prison warder who set him up.
- In spite of his threats, he obtains no useful information about the other conspirators.
- For their own safety, but also for pleasure, Reacher and Roscoe take a trip out of town to a road house.
- On their return, they discover that Roscoe's house has been invaded by the same killers who murdered the police chief and his wife.

Chapter 16

- The home invasion has disturbed Roscoe. They spend the night in a hotel.
- In the morning, they go off to work at the police headquarters.
- Kliner is hanging around at the police headquarters.
- Reacher continues to speculate about the link between the conspiracy and his brother's death. The link is obviously to do with money, since Joe worked for the Treasury.
- Roscoe promises to give Reacher a gun. She's hiding one that belonged to Gray, Finlay's predecessor as Head Detective.
- According to Finlay, a colleague of Joe's at the Treasury, called Molly, has agreed to release details of Joe's activities if Reacher will call her himself.
- Finlay, Roscoe and Reacher agree other angles of investigation, which are aimed at tracing Joe's accommodation and car.
- Reacher returns to the pathologist. The sadistic violence inflicted on Morrison corresponds to the threats received by Hubble. So, the murder is clearly linked to the conspiracy that Hubble described.

- The pathologist also reviews the physical characteristics of the second body, Sherman Stoller, speculating that he was a lorry driver.
- Reacher makes a breakthrough in the investigation of Joe's work. Molly, the colleague from the Treasury, explains that Joe was an expert on counterfeiting.
- Kliner is seen at the police headquarters. Reacher and he exchange aggressive remarks.
- Outside the barber's shop, one of the old barbers warns Reacher that some Hispanic thugs are asking after him.
- The other barber discusses the mayor and Kliner. Money is being pumped into all the town's businesses.

Chapter 17
- Reacher goes to see Hubble's employer, discovering that he had lost his job some time ago.
- Information is forthcoming on Hubble's expertise and probable role in the conspiracy. He was an expert on obtaining supplies of paper money.
- Apart from Finlay and Roscoe, the Margrave police are busy with their hunt for Morrison's killer.
- Reacher tries to follow up on his findings about Hubble by calling Charlie, but she has her phone off.
- New information about Sherman Stoller confirms that he was a lorry driver. He was apparently involved with powerful people, since a top-flight lawyer defended him after a routine traffic stop.
- Finlay has traced what is probably Joe's car. He and Reacher go to see the burned wreck.
- Back at the police headquarters, Roscoe gives Reacher a gun as promised – an enormous Desert Eagle.
- Reacher spots some suspicious Hispanic men in a car outside the police headquarters.
- He discusses with Finlay the fact that he's being followed. They rule out the idea that it's the FBI.
- Roscoe has been trying to find out where Joe got his car from.

- Reacher leaves the police headquarters and is followed by the Hispanic men.

Chapter 18

- Reacher sets an ambush for the two Hispanic men and kills them.
- He discovers the prison warder, Spivey, dead in the trunk of their car.
- Reacher follows up with Molly again. Joe was involved in the prevention of fake-currency importation.
- Reacher disposes of the bodies of the two Hispanic men in an airport car park.
- Reacher and Roscoe track down what they think is Sherman Stoller's house. Actually, it's his parents' address.
- They go to the actual home address of Stoller – a suspiciously plush apartment.
- Stoller's girlfriend says she believes he was stealing.
- The cargoes he was carrying consisted of air-conditioning units.
- Reacher asks her about the word 'pluribus', but she knows nothing.
- She shows them a picture of her partner that has Hubble in the background.
- Roscoe has seen something else in the picture but doesn't immediately explain what.

Chapter 19

- Roscoe explains that the door shown in the photo is recognisable as one at Kliner's warehouse.
- Roscoe links the vehicle in the photo to a company owned by Kliner.
- They will need information from either Molly at the Treasury or Picard at the FBI to make further progress with their inquiries.
- They spend the night together at a hotel.
- They wait for Picard or Molly to call.

- They discuss the Desert Eagle and its former owner, Roscoe's dead colleague Gray.
- We hear how Gray was meticulous and would probably have details of Joe's investigation somewhere.
- Finlay calls with details of Joe's rental car and accommodation, obtained from Picard. They have to go to the FBI office to pick it up.
- They pick up the information at the FBI office and go to the hotel room Joe occupied.
- En route, they spot the black pickup again.
- They've been beaten to the hotel room by some Hispanic men.
- Reacher guesses where the Hispanic men will have disposed of Joe's luggage. In the luggage, they find the other half of the piece of paper that was hidden on Joe's body.

Chapter 20
- Finlay calls. A meeting with Molly has been organised at which she will share new evidence.
- The jottings on Joe's piece of paper put the word 'pluribus' into context. It's the name of the operation: 'E Unum Pluribus'.
- It is the Latin tag used on American money, but in reverse order. Why?
- The paper also bears several other phone numbers. Whose?
- Reacher and the others leave for the appointment with Molly. The black pickup shows itself again.
- At the airport, Molly is spotted but goes missing. She is murdered before they can meet properly.
- Before she dies, Molly is able to communicate the fact that Sunday is a critical day for the conspiracy.

Chapter 21
- The death of Molly has taken Reacher's desire for revenge to a new level.

- Molly's evidence documents have been stolen, but the dead cop Gray's exhaustive case notes may contain the information they need.
- Reacher and Roscoe check out Gray's records.
- Some important files are missing, but Reacher realises that the box in which Gray stored his gun may have a further significance.
- The box does in fact contain a hidden key.
- Reacher takes the key to the barber shop, convinced that they will be able to help. They knew and liked Gray.
- The barbers hand over Gray's missing files, but only when asked by Roscoe.
- The files contain an account of unsolved homicides in New Orleans. The evidence trail in those cases led to Kliner.
- Considering the evidence so far available, Reacher concludes that the conspiracy relates to the laundering of counterfeit money.
- Gray observed a network of trucks moving cash about.
- The significance of the Sunday deadline becomes clear. A shipment will be happening.

Chapter 22

- A night passes and Reacher makes another visit to the pathologist. It seems Gray didn't commit suicide at all but died at someone else's hand. Given the circumstances on the night of his death, it looks like members of the police department were involved.
- Finlay must have got his job as head detective because he was in a personal crisis at the time. The police chief and mayor of Margrave clearly thought he would fail to investigate their criminal circle.
- Reacher also realises that every business in the town is being used to launder the money from the counterfeiting conspiracy.
- Back at the police headquarters, Finlay tells Roscoe that she needs to stand in for Picard at the safe house.

Chapter 23

- Reacher conducts surveillance at the warehouse, hoping to verify Gray's theory that it is a hub for counterfeit money shipments.
- While watching, he encounters a hobo who gives him a strange story about seeing a space ship and cops at the warehouse.
- Reacher observes trucks coming and going.
- He follows a truck for hundreds of miles before breaking into it. The truck is empty.

Chapter 24

- Reacher drives back to the police headquarters and has a verbal confrontation with Mayor Teale.
- Finlay reports that Picard still requires Roscoe at the safe house.
- He also explains that someone is hunting down the contacts on Joe's piece of paper and killing them.
- Reacher must get to the remaining contact quickly. He's an academic in New York.
- Reacher and Finlay conclude that the lorries are bringing something into the town, not distributing it.
- Reacher notices that another policeman, Baker, is spying on their activities.
- Finlay takes Reacher to the airport.

Chapter 25

- In New York, Joe's surviving academic contact, Professor Kelstein, is safe.
- Kelstein explains Joe's work and the political issues around counterfeit currency.
- After leaving the university, Reacher evades an ambush by some Hispanic men.
- He flies home and gets some sleep in Roscoe's parked car.
- He is spotted by Baker, the police officer suspected of spying on the investigation.
- Over a coffee, the crooked cop asks probing questions.

- Reacher deliberately tells the cop where he will be staying that night in order to bring on a confrontation.

Chapter 26

- Reacher goes to Hubble's home, where he will be staying for the night.
- He sets up an ambush.
- A team of killers arrives at night. Reacher kills them one by one.
- One of the killers is Kliner's son.
- The struggle in the pool has washed the ink off Joe's bit of paper.

Chapter 27

- Staying over at Hubble's again, Reacher ploughs through articles about counterfeiting. The nature of the conspiracy is becoming clear to Reacher.
- Waking up Finlay, he explains that the paper for the counterfeiting of hundred-dollar bills comes from bleached one-dollar bills.
- They go back to Stoller's parents' house, where Reacher thinks they'll find evidence of the counterfeiting conspiracy.
- As Reacher suspected, the parents are hiding some of the air-conditioner boxes used to transport counterfeit money.

Chapter 28

- Reacher and Finlay meet with Picard and discuss how to bring in the conspirators.
- They go to the police headquarters, where they've agreed to rendezvous with Picard and Roscoe.
- Reacher wonders who the tenth conspirator is – Hubble said there were ten people.
- The answer comes almost immediately: Picard arrives with a gun but no Roscoe.

Chapter 29

- The mayor and Kliner soon arrive too.
- Recordings of Charlie and Roscoe are played, asking Reacher to cooperate.
- Kliner reveals that Hubble is not dead. In fact, Kliner wants Reacher to tell him where Hubble is.
- Although Reacher doesn't know where Hubble is, Kliner insists that he must find him or the two women will be killed.
- Picard will be watching over Reacher. Only he knows Kliner's telephone number, so there's no point killing him.
- Reacher taunts Kliner with his son's death.

Chapter 30

- Reacher drives off with Picard and a couple of Kliner henchmen.
- He creates a trap by flattening the car tyre. While the wheel is being changed, he shoots Picard and the henchmen.

Chapter 31

- Now Reacher works out which hotel Hubble must be hiding in and traces him to a specific room.
- Reacher drives back to Margrave with Hubble.
- Having planned a rescue operation, they work together to bust Finlay out of the police headquarters.

Chapter 32

- Regrouping at the barber's shop, Reacher, Finlay and Hubble plan a raid on the Kliner warehouse, where Charlie and Roscoe are probably being held.
- Charlie has kids with her, so they must take care not to harm them.
- The barber's sister relates a story about Blind Blake. She was his girlfriend and witnessed his murder by the father of Mayor Teale.

Chapter 33

- They raid the warehouse and find an enormous pile of counterfeit money being shovelled into boxes by the captives.
- The villains are picked off one by one.
- It turns out that Picard has not been killed by Reacher after all. With extreme difficulty, he is at last dispatched.
- The victorious Reacher and friends are overwhelmed by joy.

Chapter 34

- Reacher describes how his relationship with Roscoe quickly failed. His love of freedom was primarily to blame, although Roscoe was also repelled by Reacher's violent methods.
- He leaves town as he arrived: on a bus.

1. JACK REACHER

'I'm not a vagrant. I'm a hobo. Big difference.'
- Lee Child, *Killing Floor*

There's no doubt about it. The character of Jack Reacher is one of the most compelling creations in popular fiction. As they used to say about James Bond, 'Women want to be with him, and men want to be him.' People love to spend four hundred pages in his company, and that is a big part of the success of Lee Child's books. So how does he do it?

Humanity

There's a common misconception that all you need in a good thriller hero is a character who can overcome challenges that would floor any ordinary person. It's true that many of the heroes and heroines in bestselling thriller fiction and movies answer to this description. But so do many of the heroes and heroines in uninspiring flops. In many cases, there's nothing really wrong with the concept or the writing in these unsuccessful thriller narratives, it's just that the main character lacks a certain key ingredient: a relatable sense of humanity.

The emotional high that you get from a story with a two-dimensional, invincible hero is all too ephemeral, burning itself out almost as soon as you finish the last chapter. As a result, it fails to get people reviewing or recommending, which is what an author of popular fiction should really be trying for. To achieve those things, you need a main character whose humanity speaks to the reader. Jack Reacher has that kind of viral likeability in barrel-loads.

If you had to pick one word to describe Reacher, it might be something like 'quirky'. The opening chapters of *Killing Floor* provide a steady drip-feed of charming and memorable characteristics. His possessions fit into a small evidence bag. He has 'No middle name. No address.' He uses his musical memories as an internal personal stereo. He has a store of random knowledge, such as the date and occasion when the motto of the United States was created. The list goes on.

The police interview in Chapter 2 is when the author does most of the exposition work on Reacher's quirks. It's important that this key information is given to the reader early in the story, and the interview setting makes the process feel entirely natural. Finlay asks precisely the sort of questions that are going around in our own heads as we try to work out who the mysterious narrator is.

Once the quirks have been established, Lee Child backs off and lets them sit in our imagination. They are not rammed down our throats. In Chapter 5 we hear about Reacher's quaint Oxford shoes. Then, in Chapter 16, we read that he's buying a new set of clothes to replace what he's wearing. They're just little top-ups.

There's an attractive minimalism that underlies many of these quirks. It's attractive because it taps into anxieties and dissatisfactions that many people share. We all feel, from time to time, that we have too many responsibilities and too much stuff. How wonderful it would be just to let it all go! Reacher's quirky lifestyle picks up on those kinds of thoughts without straying into social awkwardness or sermonising.

In fact, there's an earthy enjoyment of the things that he does allow into his life, whether it's coffee or lovers. 'I love coffee.' says Reacher in Chapter 4. 'Give me the chance and I drink coffee like an alcoholic drinks vodka.' This relishing of a few basic pleasures is another of his attractively human characteristics. It's always in tension with the minimalist lifestyle and the conflict that characterises his world. That tension is fascinating. A brief reflection on his release from prison typifies this effect.

> Getting out of prison is one of life's good feelings. So is not knowing what tomorrow holds. So is cruising silently down a

sunny road with a pretty woman at the wheel.

The opening phrase sets the tone by implying that prison stretches are a normal part of life. It's a perception of the world that's so grimly amusing that you can't help but go along with the alpha-male sentiments that follow – the relishing of quiet cars and pretty women. The final image of a woman at the wheel is also well judged. It heads off the idea that the opposite sex are just objects to Reacher. Appreciated for their beauty yes; objects no.

Reacher is categorically not a sexist character. In fact, his rather tender and considerate behaviour towards women is, in my view, a third personality trait that readers connect with quite strongly on a human level. Although Reacher notices Roscoe's physical attractiveness, he goes out of his way not to make her feel self-conscious.

> Her laugh was great. I wanted to look at her nameplate over her shirt pocket. But I didn't want her to think I was looking at her breasts.

This combination of sentiments gives him a red-bloodedness that is probably attractive to many readers. But it avoids the creepy or disrespectful undertones that could be associated with a male sexual gaze.

Reacher also treats Roscoe as a professional equal. In fact, early in the novel, he acknowledges his indebtedness, since it was her who finally got him off the hook.

> 'Thank you,' I said. 'I mean it. You worked hard to help me out.'
> She waved away my thanks with a blush and a small gesture and just drove on.

He shares investigative tasks with Roscoe, and allows her insights to guide his actions. For example, it was Roscoe who developed the theory that Kliner's warehouse was the heart of a logistics network. Reacher simply ran with it by carrying out surveillance on the premises. It's impossible to overstate how important gestures like this are to the predominantly female readership of thriller novels in creating relatability.

Heroism

Human relatability may be the key to success for thriller heroes and heroines, but the context for that is struggle and triumph. A thriller writer's job may be to create a likeable character (or at least a fascinating one), but they then have to set about torturing them. Deliberately making your beloved main character suffer does not come easily to some novice writers, but it must be mastered. Important as the quality of human relatability is, even that will become dull if it's not tested and put in peril. Furthermore, challenges force your character to rise above the mundane, and that is an inspiring thing for readers. At its best, it can fill us with a sense of possibility and hope. In *Killing Floor*, Jack Reacher encounters a truly comprehensive set of challenges, and the result is a satisfying display of exceptional qualities. These challenges fall into three main categories: mysteries, conflicts and ordeals.

Let's take those categories one at a time – firstly mysteries. When Reacher becomes involved in the police investigation, he reveals a level of competence that puts him in the Sherlock Holmes league. In fact, in a tongue-in-cheek gesture by the author, Holmes is subtly alluded to. 'Elementary' says Finlay when Reacher has concluded a lengthy (and accurate) account of the cop's past life, all based on deduction. The same extraordinary ability is on display when Reacher puts forward a theory about the first murder. He points out, for Finlay's benefit, that it must have been committed by three men. In Chapter 8, his sharp investigative mind is doing its stuff once again. He notices that a report on the fingerprints of a murder victim has come back much more quickly than the report on his own fingerprints. It's an oddity that points to some kind of official conspiracy.

There's a huge amount of variety in the types of mystery encountered by Reacher. Some are almost frivolous – tasks as pedestrian as analysing his brother's use of the apostrophe (in Chapter 27). But others are like tight knots combining several threads. A good example is the problem of finding Gray's lost case notes in Chapter 21. Some of the mysteries are intellectual. Reacher is capable of understanding the fine technical detail of counterfeiting, for example. But some are highly practical, such as the task of tracking down Hubble in a big city. In short, Reacher is like a Swiss Army knife of mystery-solving capabilities, and, as a result, we find him more and more engaging.

Now let's consider the second type of challenge that comes Reacher's way: conflict. He's in a more or less continuous state of conflict throughout the novel – first with the town authorities of Margrave, then with a group of criminal conspirators who overlap with them. He's arrested at gunpoint, subjected to a searching interrogation, attacked in prison, tailed, engaged in verbal sparring, visited by a death squad, targeted by armed kidnappers, driven around at the point of a gun and engaged in a full-scale shootout. Many of these situations call for violence.

Violence in fiction is always stylised, and the 'rules of representation' are different in the work of each author. Jack Reacher's brand of violence is ultra-ruthless. The blinding of an Aryan Brotherhood member in prison is a particularly gory and enjoyable example. It's one of several occasions when our attention is drawn to Reacher's lack of remorse after a killing.

> I didn't feel much at all. Nothing, in fact. No guilt, no remorse. None at all. I felt like I'd chased two roaches around that bathroom and stomped on them. But at least a roach is a rational, reasonable, evolved sort of a creature. Those Aryans in that bathroom had been worse than vermin. I'd kicked one of them in the throat and he had suffocated on his smashed larynx. Well, tough shit. He started it, right? Attacking me was like pushing open a forbidden door. What waited on the other side was his problem. His risk. If he didn't like it, he shouldn't have pushed open the damn door. I shrugged and forgot about it.

The level of violence in a novel is always a difficult balance to strike. Lee Child is careful to ensure that the violence dished out in *Killing Floor* remains acceptable to his readers. He does this by making sure that we share the principled outrage that drives Reacher to acts of murderous brutality. Perhaps disturbingly, a reader will countenance almost any level of cruelty if they are in sympathy with a hero's cause. Reacher's reflection on the killing of the Kliner boy is a good example of how that's done.

> The books I used to read, the movies people see, I should have fought him nobly. I was here to stand up for my brother. And right in front of me was the guy who'd kicked his body around like a bundle of rags. We should have duked it out, face to face. He should have been made aware of who his opponent was. He should have been made aware of why he had to die. All that

22

noble, man-to-man stuff. But real life wasn't like that. Joe would have laughed at all that.

I swung the sap with all my strength at his head.

There's one sentence of brutal violence, but it's preceded by a mini-sermon on the subject of fairness when it comes to punishing scumbags. It's really Lee Child addressing us, asking us to go along with the violence that's about to happen. Imagine if someone had killed your last surviving relative and brutalised the body, he seems to say. Wouldn't you want to kill them in the most medieval way possible? Crunch!

Given that violence is such a well-trodden path in thriller fiction, it's important to explore unexpected aspects of conflict if possible. Reacher does have a distinctive element to his personal armoury. It's not just raw violence that brings him through his conflicts, it's also psychological strength. That's very much on display when he and Roscoe discover in Chapter 16 that they've received a visit from a team of sadistic killers. Reacher works himself up to a state of invincible self-belief. It's intended to carry Roscoe with him.

> She looked at me. I wanted her to see this huge guy. A soldier for thirteen long years. A bare-knuckle killer. Icy blue eyes. I was giving it everything I had. I was willing myself to project all the invincibility, all the implacability, all the protection I felt. I was doing the hard, no-blink stare that used to shrivel up drunken marines two at a time. I wanted Roscoe to feel safe. After what she was giving me, I wanted to give her that. I didn't want her to feel afraid.

By showing us characters whose behaviour under stress is the exact opposite to Reacher's, Lee Child highlights the exceptional nature of his hero. Consider Roscoe's response to the same home invasion.

> The defenses crashed down. She pressed herself into the corner by the door. Tried to flatten herself onto the wall. Stared into space like she was seeing all the nameless horrors. Started crying like her heart was broken. I stepped over and held her tight. Pressed her against me and held her as she cried out the fear and the tension. She cried for a long time. She felt hot and weak. My

shirt was soaked with her tears.

Reacher not only has impregnable inner defences, but also an ability to wage psychological warfare. He's able to intimidate opponents with a powerful force of character. Think of his nose-to-nose encounter with Kliner towards the end of the novel. Having calculated that his best chance in a near-hopeless situation is to get into his opponent's head and go for a weak spot, he taunts Kliner with the suspicion that his son may be dead.

> I leaned forward and stared right into his eyes.
> 'Can't your son get him for you?' I said, quietly.
> Nobody spoke. I leaned forward some more.
> 'Tell your boy to go pick him up,' I said.
> Kliner was silent.
> 'Where's your son, Kliner?' I asked him.
> He didn't say anything.
> 'What happened to him?' I said. 'Do you know?'
> He knew, but he didn't know. I could see that. He hadn't accepted it. He'd sent his boy after me, and his boy hadn't come back. So he knew, but he hadn't admitted it to himself. His hard face went slack. He wanted to know. But he couldn't ask me. He wanted to hate me for killing his boy. But he couldn't do that either. Because to do that would be to admit it was true.
> I stared at him. He wanted to raise that big shotgun and blow me into a red dew. But he couldn't. Because he needed me to get Hubble back. He was churning away inside. He wanted to shoot me right then. But forty tons of money was more important to him than his son's life.
> I stared into his dead eyes. Unblinking. Spoke softly.
> 'Where's your son, Kliner?' I said.
> There was silence in the office for a long time.
> 'Get him out of here,' Kliner said. 'If you're not out of here in one minute, Reacher, I'll shoot the detective right now.'

Now we come to the third type of challenge faced by Reacher. In the course of the novel, he undergoes at least one major psychological ordeal: his imprisonment. This episode is perhaps the most malicious torture inflicted by Lee Child on his character. After all, what would challenge a rootless wanderer more than the loss of their freedom? Reacher rises above the ordeal through self-mastery and resilience. The seriousness of the challenge is clearly established in the way the prison environment is described.

> The walls looked massively thick. Like a dungeon. Above my head was a low concrete ceiling. The cell didn't feel like a room bounded by walls, floor, ceiling. It felt like a solid block of masonry with a tiny living space grudgingly burrowed in.

The sense of claustrophobia is powerful. It really makes us understand Reacher's aversion to cages.

But it's equally clear that imprisonment is not going to get the better of Jack Reacher. During his incarceration at the police headquarters, he reveals an interesting technique that lets him rise above his surroundings: he 'plays' music to himself from his internal store of favourite tracks. It's obviously something that has got him through bad times in the past.

> To calm down, I ran music through my head. The chorus in 'Smokestack Lightning.' The Howling Wolf version puts a wonderful strangled cry on the end of the first line. They say you need to ride the rails for a while to understand the traveling blues. They're wrong. To understand the traveling blues you need to be locked down somewhere. In a cell. Or in the army. Someplace where you're caged. Someplace where smokestack lightning looks like a faraway beacon of impossible freedom. I lay there with my coat as a pillow and listened to the music in my head. At the end of the third chorus, I fell asleep.

The references to the army and lock downs hint at life experiences that have given him great mental strength.

Now that we have an understanding of the three types of challenge encountered by Reacher, let's look at how Lee Child focuses and concentrates the hero's struggles to give the reader a really satisfying experience.

It's crucial to the success of any thriller that the hero goes through his darkest hours in the final few chapters, and *Killing Floor* does not disappoint. The challenges encountered by Reacher become more and more intense and comprehensive until they hit a peak of difficulty in Chapter 29. The complexity of his problems at this point almost defies description. But let me try anyway. Here goes! He has to save Roscoe and Charlie by finding Hubble, even though he has already failed in that task over nineteen chapters, and in spite of the fact that Picard is watching over him, and in spite of the fact that he has to report to Kliner by a certain time, and in spite of the fact that his only means of communicating with Kliner is Picard, who has the mobile phone number in his head. Phew!

Faced with this swarm of interconnected challenges at the climax of the novel, Reacher's response is to sit down to a meal and have a think. Meanwhile the reader is thinking too: How on earth is Reacher going to get out of this one? The pause for thought lends emphasis to the difficulty of the challenge while also building suspense. The solution that he comes up with is appropriately satisfying. It involves the quality of cunning, because he deliberately damages the car he and Picard are travelling in. It involves violence, because he has to gun down Picard and the other henchmen. But most spectacularly, it involves Sherlock-Holmes-like powers of deduction as he draws on years of military-policing experience to identify Hubble's likely location.

One final note on the subject of heroism. In life, nobody is perfect, and we tend to secretly dislike individuals who set themselves up as paragons. In fiction – especially thriller fiction – it's different. We want the main character in a thriller to have capabilities that are well beyond our own – not superpowers as such, but definitely elite-level capabilities. It's important to realise, however, that a character can and should make mistakes from time to time. Even the great Jack Reacher trips up at least once in *Killing Floor*. He may possess the investigative insight of Sherlock Holmes, but he still manages to falsely conclude that Hubble has been murdered. Perfection is boring, and one of the best ways of making life tougher for your fictional creation is to have them screw up. Struggle is, after all, the essence of thriller writing.

Character-Saturated Viewpoint

Most of the character insights described above are delivered in a direct way, through actions and dialogue. But there's another way that Reacher's character is communicated to us, and it's so subtle that you may not even be aware of it as you're reading. That's because it relates to the way we actually perceive the fictional world. We see it, hear it, smell, it, touch it and taste it exclusively through Reacher's senses and words. Reacher (or rather Lee Child channelling Reacher) decides what we experience and how we experience it. As a result, our viewpoint is saturated with his personality. As readers, we absorb that personality almost subliminally.

Lee Child famously writes some of his books in the first person, adopting Reacher's viewpoint, and some in the third person, describing Reacher's actions from the outside. Although it's possible to reproduce this character-saturated viewpoint in a third-person narration, it's undoubtedly easier in the first person, which gives a much more intimate encounter with the viewpoint character. It's no surprise that this first novel in the Jack Reacher series is in the first person.

The character-saturated viewpoint is a great way of quickly and flexibly conveying many different facets of the same personality. In Chapters 1 to 4, Reacher's perceptions unmistakably reveal a military and policing background as he registers the capabilities of the arrest team and their weapons. But, moments later, we find him enjoying the physical attractiveness of a woman, then reading the psychology of his interviewer by noting his body language, then taking a dislike to Hubble, the yuppie. And so on. Layer by layer, the author builds up a varied and complex picture of Reacher's personality.

Reacher's perceptions are not static either. They change over time. During his arrest, he understandably has an extremely negative perception of the police headquarters. At the start of Chapter 2, he remarks on the harsh look of the place. It seems like an impersonal and intimidating environment.

> Inside it was cool again. Everything was white and chrome. Lights were fluorescent. It looked like a bank or an insurance office. There was carpet. A desk sergeant stood behind a long reception counter. The way the place looked, he should have said: how may I help you, sir? But he said nothing. He just looked at me. Behind him was a huge open-plan space.

This perception changes markedly as Reacher finds that he can make life difficult for Finlay, the interviewing detective. By the end of Chapter 3, he's sitting down with a newspaper, taking in the sunny weather outside and the buzz in the police headquarters.

> Behind the desk sergeant the uniformed woman who'd printed me was busy. Keyboard work. The large room was quiet but it

hummed with the energy of investigation.

To give you an idea of how effective the character-saturated viewpoint is as a technique, compare it with the following paragraph, which conveys the same information more directly.

> They were underestimating me in a big way. I had told them I had been a military policeman. Maybe they believed me, maybe they didn't. Maybe it didn't mean much to them either way. But it should. A military policeman deals with military lawbreakers. Those lawbreakers are service guys. Highly trained in weapons, sabotage, unarmed combat. Rangers, Green Berets, marines. Not just killers. Trained killers. Extremely well trained, at huge public expense. So the military policeman is trained even better. Better with weapons. Better unarmed. Baker had to be ignorant of all that. Hadn't thought about it. Otherwise he would have had a couple of shotguns aimed at me for the trip to the bathroom. If he thought I was their guy.

It's much less specific and leaves the reader feeling a little spoon-fed. That said, you can't convey everything about a character through the quality of the viewpoint. It would be boring and tedious. Sometimes it's just quicker and easier to say what you mean.

Voice

It's not just the content of Reacher's observations that provides us with an insight into his personality, it's the tone of voice also.

The predominant tone of Reacher's narration is best described as 'hardboiled'. That term is usually used in connection with early-twentieth-century writers such as Dashiell Hammett and Raymond Chandler, and it is often misunderstood. Some people use it to refer to the whole genre of pulp detective fiction, but, in fact, it refers to the style of delivery that Hammett, Chandler and others perfected. It's characterised by

- the plain language of the ordinary man,
- terse sentences, and
- excursions into metaphor.

All those qualities are present in Reacher's delivery. Let's take a few examples.

Here's an anecdote that Reacher uses to illustrate the dangers of prison life.

> I remembered an army guy, a deserter. Young guy, not a bad recruit, went AWOL because he got some nut religion. Got into trouble in Washington, demonstrating. Ended up thrown in jail, among bad guys like on this floor. Died on his first night. Anally raped. An estimated fifty times. And at the autopsy they found a pint of semen in his stomach. A new boy with no status. Right at the bottom of the pecking order. Available to all those above him.

Carved-up sentences and flat language are the hallmarks of the passage. The fractured sentences mimic natural speech and suggest a tough, taciturn personality. The vocabulary is also about as unvarnished as it possibly could be. The phrase 'nut religion' is the standout example. And even though he's describing a sickeningly violent event, there's no overwrought language, just bald numerical information. It's a voice that's hardened by experience.

There's one area in which Lee Child's approach differs from early-twentieth-century hardboiled style: his restrained use of metaphorical language. In the work of Chandler, the metaphors come thick and fast, and draw attention to themselves with their elaborateness. A typical example comes in *The Big Sleep*, when orchids are described as 'plants with nasty meaty fingers and stalks like the newly washed fingers of dead men'. In *Killing Floor*, metaphors and similes are rarer and generally more low-key. For example, Reacher describes, with great economy, the effect of firing the Desert Eagle.

> My right arm was sore. Like somebody had hit my palm with a hammer.

There are more elaborate metaphors, but these are few and far between. For example, in Chapter 19, Reacher describes an attractive view with unexpected rhetorical flair.

> The cars in the lots caught the sun and looked like jewels on beige velvet. The planes clawed their way into the air and wheeled slowly away like fat, important birds. The buildings downtown grew tall and straight in the sun. A glorious morning.

A couple of other similes, in Chapter 26, have an almost gothic quality that makes them leap off the page. The phrases in question are 'like a ghost from hell' and 'like banshees'. They're used in the context of the ambush at the Hubble residence. Their combined effect is to heighten the drama of a scene that's already emotionally charged. They wouldn't look out of place in a Chandler novel, but, in *Killing Floor*, they're exceptions.

An occasional but significant feature of Reacher's voice is its humorousness – a quality that goes a long way to making anyone likeable. In Chapter 1, he dismisses the arresting officers with a few sarcastic words.

> I wasn't going to lie on the floor. Not for these country boys. Not if they brought along their whole police department with howitzers.

The humour isn't really seen in Reacher's interactions with other characters. It's just for us the readers. That feels special – like we're being let into a private world. Consider a passage towards the end of the novel.

> 'Get dressed, Finlay,' I said again. 'Got to go.'
> He grunted, but he went to get dressed. Took him a while. Fifteen minutes, maybe. He disappeared into the bathroom. Went in there looking like a normal sort of a guy, just woken up. Came out looking like Finlay. Tweed suit and all.

He shares a private joke with us, but the interaction with Finlay is totally straight-faced.

Personality Before Everything

The first four chapters of this thirty-four-chapter book are really one long introduction to the character of Jack Reacher – an important chance to spend some time in his company before the plot starts to pick up steam.

Allowing the reader to get comfortable with Reacher's personality is even more important to the author than giving us his basic biographical details. We don't, for example, learn Reacher's name until Chapter 3. The only physical description of him that we ever receive is in Chapter 2, and that's delivered in an indirect fashion, by comparing him with someone else.

The getting-to-know-you period is so important that Reacher doesn't engage in much activity while it's on-going. He doesn't become truly active until it looks like he might be dragged off to prison. At that point, he starts trying to help Finlay exonerate him. Normally, it's important for the main character in a novel to be the most active character, but here we have a long period of seemingly deliberate passivity. He's arrested, put in a cell, asked a lot of questions by another character and left in the cell while other inquiries take place. It represents a huge risk on Lee Child's part. The danger is that Reacher will look weak and unconvincing. But the risk clearly paid off, since readers took the character to their hearts almost immediately.

Without this 'speed-dating' introduction to Reacher's background and personality in the opening four chapters, the reader wouldn't be prepared for his 'larger-than-life' exploits later in the novel. They would ring utterly hollow. Imagine if we knew nothing about Reacher's military background, and then, in Chapter 25, we saw him set an ambush for Kliner's henchmen and pick them off one by one. It would seem absurd, even if an explanation of Reacher's deadly professionalism were subsequently provided. Part of the joy of a scene like the ambush at the Hubble house is the reader's anticipation of the action that's going to unfold. As a writer, you can only get the reader's mouth watering if you give them a sniff of the cooking. So, don't be lazy or tardy with your exposition of the main character's capabilities.

Takeaway

- Human qualities make for a memorable main character.
- In *Killing Floor*, Reacher's appealing humanity has various strands.
    - o Quirky minimalism
    - o Relishing basic pleasures
    - o Showing tenderness and respect towards women
- The heroic aspect of Jack Reacher's character is highlighted by the many challenges that come his way. These fall into three categories.
    - o Mysteries
    - o Conflicts

- o Ordeals
- A character-saturated viewpoint is a great way of revealing a multi-dimensional and constantly changing personality.
- The voice of Jack Reacher contributes to our sense of his personality. It's hardboiled but humorous.
- Establishing Reacher's personality is the absolute priority in Chapters 1 to 4, even at the expense of action.

2. GOOD AND EVIL

'Bad people, Reacher. These are bad people. As bad as they come.'
- Lee Child, *Killing Floor*

Thriller narratives are battles waged on a moral landscape. At their heart, in most cases, there is a very basic pattern: the world is put out of joint by characters who indulge in some form of destructive behaviour, then the world is fixed by other characters who have the means to impose a form of order. Often, the new order is not at all the same as the original order.

When you sit down to plan a thriller, one of the best ways to begin the story-design process is to consider what type of destructive behaviour takes place to set your plot in motion. Secondarily, you need to plan how your various characters are going to tend either to disorder or order. To help you get to grips with that complex process, and hopefully form an understanding of the forces that drive it, we're going to consider how Lee Child has structured the moral landscape of *Killing Floor*.

Evil that Affects Individuals

Usually, the very first thing that you read in a crime thriller is a description of some criminal activity or its aftermath. There is one thing, above all else, that the writer must achieve as they describe the crime and the various responses to it: they must make the reader understand that the crime just committed was a tear in the fabric of the fictional world so bad that it needs to be fixed by an exceptional individual. That is my understanding of the term 'evil' in the context of a crime thriller.

There's a reason why murder is the crime of choice for thrillers. It's because killing is considered the ultimate taboo – the greatest tear in the fabric of the world – and, as a result, it tends to hook readers very effectively. The mind of every civilised human being is programmed to respond with tingling horror even to fictional accounts of murder. That's why, when you read the opening sections of a crime thriller, you receive an emotional impetus that usually carries you right to the end of the story.

Killing Floor does not begin with an account of the first murder, but it does begin with a description of the ripples going out into the world – in other words, Reacher's arrest. There's a good reason why Lee Child chooses to start in this way. It's because the energy that readers get from a description of a murder is even more powerful if the victim is either highly likeable or closely linked to a likeable character. As we saw in the last chapter, the author goes to enormous lengths to make readers fall in love with Jack Reacher at the start of *Killing Floor*. And he's very successful. So, when we learn in Chapter 9 that his brother, Joe, has been murdered, we get a correspondingly huge emotional rush. From that point on, we are rooting for Reacher to identify and wreak revenge on the killer.

According to the standard murder narrative that I described, this emotional rush should carry us right to the end of the novel. But, surprisingly, that's not quite what happens. Given that so much emotion is riding on Reacher's revenge mission, it's slightly strange that, later in the novel, the idea of revenge doesn't seem foremost in his mind – not even at those moments when you would expect it to be, namely the scenes when he kills. The revenge mission is really only hinted at in passing on those occasions. In Chapter 18, for example, Reacher spares no more than a brief thought for his brother as he guns down two Kliner henchmen.

> The bullets had made quite a mess. I looked down at the two guys in the silence and thought about Joe.

Even this cursory reflection is somewhat vague and unfocused. What exactly was he thinking about Joe? Did the henchmen's injuries remind him of those inflicted on his brother? Did the killing feel like justice done? It's not clear.

The only moment when Reacher clearly reflects on the link between a killing and Joe's death is during the ambush at the Hubble house in Chapter 26.

> I shut my eyes for a second and pictured Joe lying on the slab at the morgue with no face. Pictured Roscoe shaking with horror as she stared at the footprints on her hallway floor. Then I crashed out of the bushes. Skipped up behind the guy. Smashed the sap across the back of his skull.

The sentiment is almost lost in the action, and it doesn't even relate to one of the key people behind Joe's death. It seems like a pretty low-key howl of revenge.

This strange absence of vengeful thoughts demands explanation. To my mind, it's almost as though Joe's murder has served its story purpose by Chapter 10. It motivated Reacher to stay put in Margrave and persuaded the reader to invest emotionally in the investigation, but with those objectives completed, Lee Child seems to put the revenge mission on a back burner and turn the emotional temperature down.

In the final chapter of the novel, Reacher actually acknowledges that his motives for bringing down the criminals were mixed.

> I felt somehow I'd done it all for her and Joe. I hadn't done it because I had wanted to do it. It was Joe's business and it was her town and these were her people. I'd done it because I'd seen her trying to melt into her kitchen wall, crying like her heart was breaking. I'd done it for Joe and Molly. At the same time as feeling I needed no justification at all, I had been justifying it to myself like that.
> …
> The whole thing had gotten out of hand. Before, it had all been about Joe. It had been private. Now it was public.

It's clear that, during the middle chapters of the novel, revenge is not the only emotional factor driving Reacher and the reader. In Chapter 11, for example, we hear about the murder of the police chief and his wife. That pair of killings is characterised by a shocking ultra-violence that engages Reacher's investigative mind and fills us with horror-fascination. The author even returned to it in Chapter 16, at the pathologist's office, encouraging us to revel in the gory details for a second time.

> 'The man was nailed to the wall, technically to the floor also, through the feet. His genital area was attacked. The scrotum was severed. Postmortem evidence suggests that the woman was persuaded to swallow the amputated testicles.'

As the revenge motive is quietly side-lined, it's the sadism of the murders that's now being presented as the essence of evil – as the biggest tear in the fabric of the fictional world. Why?

Engaging the reader's emotions and keeping them gripped for four hundred pages is tough. In traditional thrillers, a convincing murder and an interesting or likeable victim were enough. But in contemporary thriller novels and movies, those things no longer grip readers or instil in them a powerful desire for justice. The reader response, such as it is, just doesn't take them all the way to the end of the story. There has to be a special, high-octane fuel additive to do that. The response of many authors is to use the shock-horror tactic of ingenious sadism.

There are alternatives. Let's consider the approach taken by two other influential thriller writers. *Roseanna*, the first novel by pioneering Swedish crime writers Maj Sjöwall and Per Wahlöö, concerns itself exclusively with one murder – the killing of a young woman whose body is dredged up from a canal. Such shocks as the story provides are mainly related to the salacious details of the victim's sex life and the appearance of her body when it emerges from the water. The interest is sustained by providing the reader with an entertaining cast of characters, and by showing us that the investigators are emotionally involved in the case.

The James Bond novels by Ian Fleming are my second example of an alternative to explicit violence. They deal with life and death situations, but it's not blood and guts that grip the reader, it's the personality and consumption habits of the legendary British spy. Another important factor is the exotic and grandiose nature of Fleming's villains.

I'm not passing judgement on Lee Child for resorting to ultra-violence. After all, *Roseanna* and the James Bond novels were written several decades before *Killing Floor*, and society has well and truly succumbed to blood lust in the meantime. But I think it is important for writers to understand that there are alternatives when it comes to creating villains and crimes that are truly gripping.

Evil that Affects Society

Murder – the ultimate crime against the individual – provides the emotional energy for *Killing Floor*. But, behind that, there is another crime: an ingenious plan for turning one-dollar notes into hundred-dollar notes. You could call it a crime against society, rather than the individual.

'Crime against society' may sound an odd description, but that's clearly how the author wants us to see it. He goes out of his way to make us understand that the social consequences of large-scale counterfeiting are potentially cataclysmic. In Chapter 18, Molly explains to Reacher how fake money undermines a country's internal and external relationships.

> 'Difficult to describe,' Molly said. 'It's all about trust and faith. It's almost metaphysical. If foreign markets are getting flooded with fake dollars, that doesn't really matter in itself. But if the people in those foreign markets find out, then it does matter. Because they panic. They lose their faith. They lose their trust. They don't want dollars anymore.'

The phrase 'Faith and trust' echoes through the novel. For example, in Chapter 25, Reacher visits Professor Kelstein, another expert in the field of counterfeiting. The elderly academic explains how imports of fake money are akin to an act of war. They originate from the darkest corners of the world and are sometimes sponsored by enemy governments because of their corrosive effect. Reacher immediately recalls Molly's words about 'Faith and trust'.

But there's a problem with these attempts to clarify exactly why counterfeiting is an economy-wrecking tear in the fabric of national life. They're totally uncompelling! Yes, we can accept on an intellectual level that fake money is a threat to society, but we just aren't emotionally caught up in it. There are two reasons for that. Firstly, the lengthy exposition sessions with Molly and Kelstein are devoid of actual, tangible evidence. They are just words from the big chair, and if readers wanted that they would have read an encyclopaedia. In fiction argument must come through action. Secondly, there is a problem with counterfeiting as a subject for a crime thriller: it's not emotive in the way that murder is. I don't think I'm alone in finding it quite difficult to become fearful or outraged over it.

Given the shortcomings of counterfeiting as an expression of evil, we have to ask ourselves why it's in the novel at all. If you take nothing away from this book, remember the following dictum: well-written works of popular fiction are highly economical creations in which everything serves some purpose. So, what purpose does the counterfeiting conspiracy serve in *Killing Floor*?

We can begin to answer that question if we look at how the counterfeiting conspirators are depicted in the novel. Long before we become aware of the nature of their criminal activities, the author is putting a lot of energy into showing how unlikeable they are as people. The repellent qualities ascribed to them tell us a lot about the significance of their counterfeiting activities.

In Chapter 9, for example, Reacher encounters a woman drinking coffee in the same convenience store as himself. She's crying and seems to be overwhelmed with terror. Eventually, she's picked up by a man in a black pickup truck. That's Reacher's cue to start quizzing the guy serving in the convenience store.

> 'I'm a stranger in town. Kliner owns the warehouses up near the highway, right?'
> 'Right,' he said. 'And a whole lot more besides. Big deal round here, Mr. Kliner.'

The woman belongs to the Kliner family: local business magnates who own most of the town. Wealth is one of those things that we've been taught to be suspicious of in thrillers, so we're already starting to smell a rat. But in case we were in any doubt that the Kliners are no good, the convenience store guy hints at a complicated situation of domestic abuse.

> 'I've heard she don't get along so good with the kid.'
> He gave me the sort of nod that terminates casual conversations. Moved away to wipe off some kind of a chromium machine behind the other end of the counter. The black pickup was still waiting outside.

The menacing pickup says it all about the source of the woman's fear.

Significantly, the Kliner woman never makes it back into the story. That's because her job is now done, having sown the seeds of dislike for the Kliners. But the author continues to water those seeds, adding to the impression of the Kliners as a moneyed, aggressive clan. When Reacher leaves the convenience store, he's followed in a sinister way by the same black pickup, driven by the Kliner woman's stepson. In Chapter 13, the vehicle appears for a third time, and on this occasion the Kliner boy jumps out and gets into a verbal showdown with Reacher. As the argument progresses, there is absolutely no doubt that Lee Child wants us to dislike Kliner junior because of his wealth and arrogance.

> 'You're trespassing,' he said.
> 'This is your sidewalk?' I said.
> 'It sure is,' the kid said. 'My daddy's Foundation paid for every inch of it. Every brick.'

It's difficult to imagine a more childish and conceited argument. We're beginning to understand the nature of the evil that underlies the counterfeiting conspiracy.

The Kliner family are not the only conspirators who we get to know and dislike from an early stage of the novel. In Chapter 12, Finlay expresses his disillusion with the town and its mayor, Teale. This key figure in the conspiracy is described as an old-school southern reactionary.

> 'What's the story with this guy Teale?' I asked him.
> Finlay shrugged. Tried to find a way to explain it.
> 'He's just a southern asshole,' he said. 'Old Georgia family, probably a long line of southern assholes. They've been the mayors around here since the beginning. I dare say this one's no worse than the others.'

This time it's social status, rather than money, that's held up for our disapproval. Finlay hints at nepotism, abuse of power and racism without actually naming those things. Along with wealth, they are the soil from which the counterfeiting conspiracy grows.

This strategy of making the criminals in the novel as unlikeable as possible may seem a rather obvious thing for an author to do, but there are plenty of thrillers that take a different approach. Some authors choose to make the bad guys as charming as possible. In the hands of a skilled writer, that can even enhance the horror of their evil acts. The classic example of this is Hannibal Lecter, the serial killer who is the main antagonist of at least one novel by Thomas Harris, and a particularly vile anti-hero in others. A deeply cultivated and witty individual, we are attracted to him while still being repelled by his crimes.

Lee Child's approach to villainy may seem less sophisticated than that of Thomas Harris, but the two strategies have different literary functions and are equally valid. Harris's novels use murder and torture to take us deep into the dark places of the human psyche. *Killing Floor*, by contrast, uses the crime of counterfeiting to comment on social evil. This is something that he has firmly denied doing, but, in my view, each of the Jack Reacher novels has deeply political undertones.

The political undertones of *Killing* Floor should be clear to you by now. The novel depicts a world in which there is no dividing line between social evils, such as greed and bigotry, and a criminal conspiracy that damages society as a whole. That yell from the young Kliner, 'My daddy's Foundation paid for every inch of it', crystallises exactly what makes him and his kind so loathsome, but it also hints at the mechanics of the criminal conspiracy – specifically the laundering of fake money through Kliner Foundation subsidies.

There's one more aspect to the relationship between counterfeiting and social evil that needs to be touched on. As we will see in a later chapter, Lee Child is an expert at weaving metaphors into his stories, and counterfeiting seems to be one such metaphor. When you consider the essence of counterfeiting as a crime, it comes down to a simple idea: the corrupted and corrupting nature of *fake* money. But Lee Child also invites us to view counterfeiting as a metaphor for the corrupting influence of money *in general*. He wants us to see wealth and greed as forces that undermine 'Faith and trust' just as much as counterfeit money does. He achieves this by a number of ingenious means – as I will discuss in the chapter on Values and Themes – but, primarily, it's the wealth and arrogance of the key counterfeiting conspirators that suggests the interpretation.

Evil in the Shadows

Have you seen the movie *Jaws*? Or that other classic, *Alien*? On the face of it, they seem like quite different films. The first is set on a holiday island and has a police chief for a hero. His antagonist is a killer shark. The second is set on a spaceship and pits a female crew member against an alien creature. But, different as they are, *Jaws* and *Alien* basically have the same plot: there's a monster out there somewhere and it's picking people off one by one.

Killing Floor also reflects aspects of this plot structure. Like the grisly shark attacks and the slaughters carried out by the alien, the killings in Lee Child's novel take place out of sight, and their concealment contributes greatly to their sense of menace. Paid henchmen hover threateningly around the edges of scenes – nameless, voiceless men who watch and wait. The black pickup truck of Kliner junior also circles predatorially around Reacher, appearing every few chapters in the middle of an unrelated scene. You can almost imagine the famous shark theme from *Jaws* playing when it's mentioned.

Then, occasionally, the killers' handiwork shows up and hints at the appalling, sadistic actions that must have taken place. The murder of Chief Morrison and his wife is the most shocking example.

> 'OK,' he said. 'It was pretty horrible. One of the worst I've ever seen. And I've seen a few, let me tell you. I've seen some pretty bad ones, but this was something else. He was naked. They nailed him to the wall. Six or seven big carpentry nails through his hands and up his arms. Through the fleshy parts. They nailed his feet to the floor. Then they sliced his balls off. Just hacked them off. Blood everywhere. Pretty bad, let me tell you. Then they slit his throat. Ear to ear. Bad people, Reacher. These are bad people. As bad as they come.'

When, in Chapter 15, we see that Roscoe's home has been invaded by these faceless killers, in all likelihood by the same kill squad, we feel a shiver of fear, as if the Angel of Death has passed over. Extreme danger is out there somewhere, and it's all the more terrifying for being hidden.

Primal Evil

The killing of Joe, Stoller and the Morrisons may be carried out under the cover of darkness, but the public faces of the murderers are on full display throughout the novel. That is one of the most intriguing aspects of the depiction of evil in *Killing Floor*. We get to watch as ruthless killers engage in social interactions, revealing an inner foulness in spite of themselves.

We've already seen how Kliner junior gets into an aggressive showdown with Reacher, delivering that petulant line about his daddy owning the whole town, including its sidewalks. But one of the most significant aspects of this encounter has not been touched on yet. It's the fact that the Kliner boy also makes a sexual claim on Roscoe. In fact, that is really the subtext to the whole scene.

> 'But I'm not talking about the sidewalk. I'm talking about Miss Roscoe. She's mine. She's mine from when I first saw her. She's waiting for me. Five years. Five years, she's been waiting for me, until the time is right.'

This sexual-jealousy undertone puts the depiction of evil on a deeper level. It's not just about wealth and arrogance. It also feeds on deep and aggressive psychological drives, like an animal that has to lock horns with every rival it sees. This kind of primitive opposition between a main character and the forces of evil is an important part of creating a great thriller. The more basic you can make the clash, the better.

In *Killing Floor*, the primitive antipathy between Reacher and his enemies is not always so overt. Both Kliner senior and Mayor Teale make brief appearances in which all the violence is under the surface of the text. Reacher's encounters with those two characters ostensibly consist of nothing more than harsh words, but the reader knows there are unstated threats on both sides. On two occasions, the author makes us feel the presence of that hidden violence by employing a visual simile: he compares Kliner senior to a predatory animal.

> His face was lean and flat and hard. His mouth was a line carved into it. Then he moved his eyes onto me. I felt like I was being illuminated by a searchlight. His lips parted in a curious smile. He had amazing teeth. Long canines, canted inward, and flat square incisors. Yellow, like an old wolf. His lips closed again and he snapped his gaze away. Pulled the door and crunched over the gravel to his truck. Took off with the roar of a big motor and a

spray of small stones.

The fear of wolves is probably the most ancient and primitive human fear of all. Perhaps that's why it dominates European fairy tales. It's certainly why it gets invoked here as a visual metaphor for the nature of Kliner's evil.

The Moral Scale

So much for the nature of evil in *Killing Floor*. It's about rapacious greed, violence, arrogance, racism and primal jealousies. It lurks in the darkness, and, secretly, we find it quite exciting. Now we turn to the general moral landscape of the novel.

The common perception of thriller novels and movies is that they're sharply polarised into 'good guys' and 'bad guys'. But that is, in fact, a recipe for failure as a thriller writer. *Killing Floor* is much more morally complex, and that's not unusual in the genre. Imagine a moral scale with good at one end and evil at the other, where evil is the tangle of ugly traits described above, and good is the diametric opposite – a force that seeks to mend tears in the fabric of the fictional world and establish a new order. Where would you place each of Lee Child's characters on that scale? If you have time, get a pencil and paper, draw the scale and try to decide where all of the characters belong – the good end, the evil end or somewhere in between. It's not an easy task, but if you give it a go, you'll pretty quickly realise that there are characters spread all over the place, and some of them don't even finish the novel where they started.

See if you agree with my map of the novel's moral landscape.

Good Characters

One of the most striking features of *Killing Floor*'s moral scale is that there are barely any characters situated at the good extreme – the end that contradicts greed, violence and all the rest of it. In fact, I can think of only four characters who fit the description.

- Joe Reacher
- Gray
- Blind Blake

- Kelstein

Significantly, the first three are dead and the fourth not only lives far from the centre of action, in New York, but also appears in just one scene. Good has been firmly pushed to the margins of the fictional world.

It's important to note that Jack Reacher, the main character of the novel, is not at the scale's good extreme. He's certainly closer to the good end than the evil end, of course. As we've seen, he has an unmaterialistic approach to life, a respect for the opposite sex, a high regard for black blues musicians and considerable intellectual ability. Nothing could be more different from the Kliner boy, for example. But the ruthless methods Reacher employs bear an uncomfortable similarity to the methods of evil. In the process of tracking down his brother's murderer, he engages in more than a little extra-judicial killing. For that reason alone, he can hardly be considered morally equivalent to sweet old Professor Kelstein.

Anti-hero is a much-abused term, but it's actually a pretty useful label for Jack Reacher. It captures his moral ambivalence. When the term anti-hero was first coined, in the ancient world, it referred to characters who were good by the moral standards of their world, but essentially incompetent. They lacked heroic prowess but still played the central role in a story. Reacher is more typical of a modern conception of the anti-hero. He displays considerable prowess, but some of his qualities resemble evil traits. Nevertheless, he pursues goals that could be classified as good.

It's difficult to see how a pure hero could be acceptable to any twenty-first-century audience over the age of five. That's why most stories include anti-heroes these days. In many cases, the ancient-world conception of the anti-hero is revived. Crime thrillers are full of self-doubting, alcohol-abusing, boss-punching cops. Perhaps we feel drawn to such characters because they magnify our own failings and show us how to deal with them. But Reacher is another type. His mix of good-heartedness and unscrupulous methods appeals to our cynicism and our desire for vindication in a world that all too often seems loaded against us.

Given that Finlay and Roscoe explicitly approve of Reacher's ruthless anti-heroic methods, they can't claim to be wholly good either. In Chapter 16, Roscoe supplies her lover with a gun – the weapon that he uses to murder two men. She barely has anything to say when he tells her about the killings in Chapter 18. Even Molly, Joe's colleague, is willing to break Treasury rules and leak information about the case. So, like Finlay and Roscoe, she is somewhere between Reacher and Kelstein on the moral scale.

Evil Characters
At the opposite end of the novel's moral scale, there's an impressively large block of characters.

- Kliner
- Kliner junior
- Teale
- Morrison
- Spivey
- Aryan brother
- Henchman 1
- Henchman 2
- Henchman 3
- Henchman 4
- Black gang member

Ten are wrapped up in the conspiracy, but the black gang member seems to be a freelance. We've already considered the nature of the evil that the conspirators embody. But we haven't yet viewed them in the context of the whole moral landscape of the novel. The most important thing to notice is that the forces of evil feel like they outweigh the forces of good in *Killing Floor*, not only numerically, but also in terms of their power over the world of the novel. They occupy most of the positions of influence, have paid off everyone for miles around and are seemingly able to extend a tentacle into any corner of life, including a prison.

This is the stuff of noir fiction. Noir is a style of writing many readers are attracted to currently. The term refers to thriller fiction that removes all moral reference points and depicts the world as a dark place where no one can be relied on. All authority is, by definition, corrupt, and the only way of getting on is to buck the system. The noir hero doesn't subscribe to any morality that we would consider heroic, but he does have a rough and ready set of values that help him navigate the darkness. It's a literary mood that traces its roots back to pulp-fiction novels of the mid-twentieth century, as well as a host of movies from the same period. Think of the Philip Marlowe novels by Raymond Chandler, or their cinematic adaptations.

Lee Child's Margrave is precisely that sort of noir environment. Most of the authority figures are corrupt – morally and criminally. Their influence extends into the business sphere, the legal profession, banking and law enforcement. They are engaging in a crime that, as we have seen, stands as a metaphor for loss of trust. And, in the midst of this darkness, the only glimmers of real goodness are dead men. But the most important point about the dominance of evil in *Killing Floor* is that it makes for a really satisfying plot climax as we witness good beating the odds to triumph in the end.

Movers and Shakers

To make matters worse, this noirish swamp is inhabited by creatures like Picard and Baker who seem to be actively working for the good but then turn out bad. From the point of view of a noir fiction writer, moral uncertainty of this kind is even more desirable than evil that flaunts itself. That's because it creates so much more dramatic potential. Turncoats are sources of uncertainty and surprise, and that is what a thriller needs more than anything else. Without twists, a thriller is nothing.

One of the biggest twists in the plot of *Killing Floor* is the revelation, in Chapter 28, that Picard, the FBI man, is not on the side of good after all. On the contrary, he is the hired muscle for the criminals – the kidnapper of Charlie and Roscoe. Although some alert readers may have seen it coming, it is a development that puts Reacher and his allies in dreadful peril, just as they seem to be getting the better of the criminals. Compared to this dramatic turnaround, the revelation that Baker has been spying for Teale comes as less of a shock. Nevertheless, it helps to muddy the moral waters.

In some senses, the moral landscape of *Killing Floor* is a classic noir environment. But in other senses, it's not very noir at all. For example, there is at least one character who counterbalances Picard and Baker by moving out of the evil camp and migrating towards the good end of the scale: Hubble. Before the story begins, he is a full-time professional criminal, using his knowledge of the banking world to corrupt the US money supply with fake currency. And, as Reacher notes, he has the look and manner of 'a man who wallowed in the yuppie dream like a pig in shit'. That would align him with another obnoxious rich kid, Kliner junior. However, by the end of the novel, Hubble is teamed up with Reacher, and plays an active part in rescuing Finlay as well as Roscoe and his wife Charlie. This kind of redemption story is absolutely anathema to noir fiction. In the noir view of the universe, we are all being sucked down to hell eventually.

The owners of the barber's shop are another emblematic example of light dawning in the darkness of Margrave. Their journey is not a dramatic redemption like Hubble's, but rather a gradual alignment with the other good characters.

When we first encounter the barbers, in Chapter 9, they express a dislike of Kliner, in fact they won't even talk about him with Reacher. They prefer to talk about Blind Blake. Their story about the murder of the old bluesman evokes interest and sympathy from the reader, but it doesn't fully align them with the other characters at the good end of the moral scale.

In Chapter 16, one of the barbers goes a step further towards alignment with the good. He tells Reacher that if Teale were in the barber's chair he might feel like cutting his throat. However, we also hear from the barber that Margrave is being pumped full of money by the Kliner Foundation, and they are apparently as happy as anyone else to take the subsidy. In Chapter 21, though, they become active allies. They honour the request of the dead detective, Gray, by passing on a box of evidence to Roscoe.

By the end of the novel, the barbers have risen to the status of figureheads for good. Their shop is literally and metaphorically the last light burning in Margrave. The sister's account of the murder of Blind Blake in Chapter 32 – in particular the revelation that it was carried out by a member of the Teale family – fully aligns them with the efforts of Reacher, Finlay and Roscoe to bring down the current Mayor Teale, among others. Or perhaps it would be better to say that Reacher's investigation aligns itself with the civil rights struggle of the twentieth century.

Drifters

The remainder of the cast members occupy the middle ground of the moral scale. Some can be described as genuinely neutral, in that they have no real awareness of the criminal goings-on.

- The suit
- The convenience store guy
- Kliner's wife (possibly)
- Charlie (possibly)

Others know about the criminal activity but have an ambivalent moral attitude to it.

- Sherman Stoller
- Stoller's girlfriend
- Stoller's dad
- Stoller's mum

Stoller was a driver delivering fake currency packaged in air-conditioner boxes. He certainly knew about the contents of the boxes because he siphoned a few off. Although he was complicit in the crime, there's a twisted form of good in the fact that he tried to get one over on the real criminals, doing right by his family in the process. As for his girlfriend, Judy, and probably his parents too, it seems they knew Sherman was a criminal, but failed to grasp the nature of the crime.

Like the other middle-ground characters, Judy has her own agenda – she resents the fact that her bread winner is gone. Similarly, Stoller's parents have to fund their retirement, Charlie wants her husband back, Kliner's wife wants to feel safe, the convenience store guy doesn't want to be seen gossiping about the Kliners and the suit has better things to do than talk to Reacher all day. This diversity of concerns and objectives helps to dilute the impression of moral polarisation in the novel.

In general, the fascinating spread of moral positions makes the cast of *Killing Floor* an effective tool for generating conflict, mystery, plot twists and moral commentary.

Takeaway

- Murder is the ultimate taboo, so it provides the necessary kick of energy for crime thrillers. Even so, authors often feel the need to boost it with something else: violence, lifestyle, humour, etc.

- After the initial murders, ultra-violence is used to maintain the main character's motivation and the reader's attention. There are alternatives to ultra-violence.

- The crime of counterfeiting may be undramatic, but it is present in *Killing Floor* as part of a moral commentary. It is a metaphor for greed. The behaviour of the principle conspirators brings that metaphor into focus.

- The killing is done largely under a veil. Terrifying evidence shows up later, which increases the sense of menace around the bad guys.

- The author puts the clash between the main character and the antagonists on a primal level. A key conspirator is described in bestial terms.

- The characters are spread right across a moral scale ranging from very good to very bad.

- Evil seems to predominate, and betrayals create a murky moral atmosphere, but good is ultimately affirmed through redemption and triumph against the odds.

3. THE 'CAST SYSTEM'

Character is king. There are probably fewer than six books every century
remembered specifically for their plots. People remember characters.
Same with television. Who remembers the Lone Ranger? Everybody.
Who remembers any actual Lone Ranger story lines? Nobody.
- Lee Child, 'Jack Reacher', *The Lineup*, Otto Penzler Ed.

As we saw in the previous chapter, *Killing Floor* has a large cast of
characters scattered across its moral landscape. I have counted
thirty-two, but there may be some walk-on parts that I've missed.
Marshalling such large forces in the service of a single creative goal
is a challenge – rather like arranging a piece of music for orchestra.
Let's consider some of the techniques involved.

Distinctness
Lee Child does an excellent job of keeping all of the characters
distinct from one another. If you make a list of the named
characters, you will notice that there are relatively few duplicated
initials. If there is a duplication, it usually signifies kinship, as with
Roscoe and Reacher, the Kliners and the Stollers. Strangely, this is
one of the most effective techniques you can use to help readers
keep the cast of characters organised in their heads. We may labour
over the names for our beloved literary creations, but the fact is,
readers mainly register the first letter.

In addition, there are very few duplications of
characteristics between the speaking characters. There is just one

black cop, one female cop and one prison warder. The only speaking characters who do blur into one another are the men who run the barber's shop, and I believe there is a special reason for this. Their close, almost brotherly relationship is a parallel to Jack and Joe Reacher's actual brotherhood. It presents an ideal of closeness that the Reacher boys were not able to live up to. The subject of parallels and contrast within the cast of characters is discussed below.

The author also deploys a technique that is very useful for making non-speaking characters distinct and memorable. When Reacher visits Hubble's former work place, the manager is referred to as 'the suit'. This is a great label, because it captures all we need to know about the person and avoids cluttering up our memory banks with another name. It would be pointless to name him given that the suit only appears in one scene. As a bonus, the label also helps to give us a flavour of Reacher's perceptions. People who work in dull office jobs are all the same to him.

Parallels and Contrasts

Having argued that the novel contains a cast of skilfully differentiated characters, I'm now going to confuse you by pointing out that there are all sorts of parallels between characters. However, the parallels that I have in mind are not based on characteristics. They tend to revolve around behaviours. For example, in Chapter 3, we learn that Reacher has been chewed up and spat out by a tough career in law enforcement.

> 'I'm a thirty-six-year-old unemployed ex-military policeman getting called a vagrant by smug civilian bastards who wouldn't last five minutes in the world I survived.'

Then, in Chapter 11, we learn that Finlay has also been beaten down by harsh experiences at the coal face of policing, paying a high personal cost.

> I thought about twenty years in Boston. Working around the clock in that busy old city. Grimy nineteenth-century precincts. Overloaded facilities. Constant pressure. An endless parade of freaks, villains, politicians, problems. Finlay had done well to survive.

51

Reacher's wandering lifestyle also parallels the wandering lifestyle of Blind Blake. The sense of kinship is so close, Reacher's self-description – 'No middle name. No address' – could almost be a line from a blues song. In fact, Reacher strongly hints that he feels this bond with Blind Blake.

> The black road blasted heat at me. Blind Blake had walked this road, maybe in the noon heat.

But it's not just the 'good' characters in *Killing Floor* who are linked by behavioural parallels. The description of the Kliner boy ranting at Reacher in the street is strongly echoed by the description of the young Teale given by the barber's sister. The Kliner kid seems to think he owns the place, appealing to his 'daddy's' authority as he shoots his mouth off.

> 'You're trespassing,' he said.
> 'This is your sidewalk?' I said.
> 'It sure is,' the kid said. 'My daddy's Foundation paid for every inch of it.'

The young Teale behaves almost identically.

> But poor Blake was blind. Didn't see them. Just crashed into the white boy. A white boy, maybe ten years old, maybe twelve. Blake sent him flying into the dirt. White boy cut his head on a stone, set up such a hollering like you never heard. The white boy's daddy was there with him. I knew him. He was a big important man in this town. His boy was screaming fit to burst. Screaming at his daddy to punish the nigger. So the daddy lost his temper and set about Blake with his cane.

Just as commonly, we see behaviours highlighted in order to create a deliberate contrast. We have already seen how Jack and Joe Reacher's distant and affectionless brotherhood is echoed and contradicted by the strong, almost-brotherly relationship of the barbers. And there are many other examples of the same technique. Some instances are very specific, as in the case of Hubble's and Reacher's shoes. Reacher notices that the ultra-privileged Hubble wears boat shoes, equating this with his moneyed, soft lifestyle.

> I was certain he would be wearing tan boat shoes. I made a substantial bet with myself he was wearing them without socks. This was a man who wallowed in the yuppie dream like a pig in shit.

By contrast, we hear all about Reacher's own Oxford shoes, which are robust and traditional.

> ... these were good shoes. Bought many years ago in Oxford, England. A university town near the airbase where I was stationed. Big heavy shoes with hard soles and a thick welt.

In every case, these parallels and contrasts serve a purpose that can be described as 'thematic'. By that I mean the details act as metaphors, standing for something beyond their function in the plot. For example, Hubble's and Reacher's shoes have something to say about the values that motivate both men: showy materialism versus robust, practical wisdom.

How Rounded?

When you read about characterisation in books on creative writing, you're told that you need to strive for depth and multidimensionality. We're told that you're supposed to know absolutely everything about them, even what they have in their pockets, although most of that information will never make it onto the page. But, how fleshed out and multidimensional are the characters of *Killing Floor*?

The simple answer is: not very. As in the majority of thrillers, deep and convincing characterisation is not valued for its own sake. That is a speciality of literary fiction, and we are concerned with popular fiction. A small group of characters close to Reacher are provided with back story, description of their appearance or mannerisms and even some detail concerning their inner life. By contrast, other characters are evoked with the minimum of information.

If a detail is provided about a character other than Reacher, Finlay or Roscoe, it is usually because that detail serves some aspect of plot or theme. The reason why we find out about Picard's enormous size is that he is being lined up as Reacher's opponent in an epic showdown towards the end of the story. The reason why we hear that Charlie Hubble reminds Reacher of formidable plantation owners of long ago is that Lee Child wishes to keep the idea of the civil rights struggle in the reader's mind – it is a key theme, as we will see in a later chapter.

Of course, even a thriller writer shouldn't altogether neglect those deft little strokes that help bring characters to life. In Chapter 16, for example, we meet the Yellow Springs pathologist. Reacher and Finlay have been interacting with him for several sentences by the time we receive anything like a description of him or his character. Description would only hold up story. The detail, when it comes, is a study in brevity.

> The tired man at the desk prepared to answer. Like preparing for a lecture.

The micro-portrait relies, at least in part, on a momentary observation of the mannerisms of the character: he clearly has a slightly pompous professional demeanour, since he addresses individuals as though they were a lecture audience. This telling detail is so good it makes the first sentence, with its unevocative use of the word 'tired', seem a little lazy, but everything is acceptable in the name of brevity where thriller writing is concerned.

The characterisation of Finlay and Roscoe is much more developed than that of most other characters in the cast. Only Reacher is more detailed. Because the author isn't channelling the viewpoint of Finlay or Roscoe, he can't hint at their personalities through the quality of their perceptions as he does with Reacher. Nevertheless, he calls on a number of techniques to flesh them out – some highly ingenious. For example, in the interview at the police headquarters, he has Reacher deduce Finlay's background.

> 'I know more than you think,' I said. 'I know you're a Harvard postgrad, you're divorced and you quit smoking in April.'
> Finlay looked blank.
> …
> 'How do you know that stuff?' Finlay asked me.
> He was intrigued. He was losing the game.

This clever little passage achieves two things at the same time. It gives us some exposition of Finlay's back story while also illustrating Reacher's powers as a detective. In another sequence that multi-tasks almost as skilfully, Roscoe's back story is briefly illuminated. It begins in Chapter 13, when the Kliner boy reveals a five-year passion for Roscoe.

> I'm talking about Miss Roscoe. She's mine. She's mine, right from when I first saw her.

Later, Roscoe confirms that she has received unwanted attention from the guy.

> 'And what's the story with the Kliner boy? He tried to warn me off you. Made out he had a prior claim.'
> She shuddered.
> 'He's a jerk,' she said. 'I avoid him when I can. You should do the same.'

It's a whole side of Roscoe's life that doesn't need to be addressed directly, but does contribute to our feeling for her as a person. She's clearly a standout beauty, and that can cause problems in the face-to-face setting of a small town. That information is evoked with just two phrases: 'He's a jerk ... I avoid him when I can.'

One thing to note about the characterisation of the more fleshed-out characters in *Killing Floor*, especially Roscoe and Finlay, is that the author often evokes personal qualities through action, not through direct description. It's worth observing how Lee Child does this, because it exemplifies a practice much praised by writers on creative writing. 'Show don't tell' is the phrase most often used to describe it. In other words, provide vivid, memorable evidence of a characteristic rather than making a bald assertion. It's an ideal that all writers should aim for, although, in thrillers, the pace of the story doesn't always allow for lengthy, drama-interrupting sequences that reveal character traits or back story.

Lee Child brings a light touch to 'showing' that barely holds up the narrative. For example, Finlay's obsessive and even slightly manic personality comes through in his driving. In Chapter 24, he freaks Reacher out by putting his foot down on the freeway while looking away from the road. It happens just after they've made a breakthrough in their understanding of the criminal conspiracy.

> 'Watch the road, Finlay,' I said. 'No good to anybody if you kill us

in a damn car.'

He grinned and faced forward. Jammed his foot down harder. The big police Chevy eased up over a hundred. Then he turned again and looked straight into my eyes for about three hundred yards. 'Coward,' he said.

There are two episodes in which this characteristic comes through. Both evoke it with the minimum of fuss and both have a legitimate narrative reason for referring to it.

Roscoe gets the same unfussy show-don't-tell treatment. The simple fact that she brings a coffee to Reacher, against protocol, is telling.

Probably against the fat chief's rules to bring coffee to the condemned man. It made me like her.

Roscoe is clearly an emotionally warm person, but also quite edgy. This daring side to her personality comes out in other gestures. In particular, she shows up outside the prison in Chapter 8 and whisks Reacher off in her car. What could possibly be more daring than making advances to a freshly released prisoner? This sense of character consistency across a number of actions is important. It creates believability.

But, before we get too carried away with praising the deep characterisation of Finlay and Roscoe, there is an important point to be made about it. No matter how rich and interesting it is, a large part of its function is to throw light on Reacher's character. Through Roscoe, we understand that Reacher is sexually attractive, for example. I assume that is an important consideration for a percentage of Lee Child's audience. Through Finlay, by contrast, we understand that Reacher is a great investigator, capable of discovering the truth from tiny details. It's a characteristic that will turn out to be important, when he's forced to track down Hubble with almost no information to go on.

Of the two characters closest to Reacher, Finlay seems the more fleshed-out and fascinating. Why is that? It's not because we receive more detail about him compared to Roscoe. We receive approximately the same level of information about both characters' backgrounds, appearance and personalities. It's also not because Finlay is more active than Roscoe. Both characters engage with the investigation in an energetic way without ever detracting from

Reacher's lead role. The real differentiator is Finlay's inner tension. His character contains conflicts in a way that Roscoe's doesn't. For example, his instinct, when it comes to policing, is to go by the book, but he knows his crooked colleagues and superiors can't be brought down by conventional means. He warns Reacher not to take matters into his own hands.

> 'You're going to feel pretty bad, and you're going to want to see justice done, but I don't want any independent action going on here, OK? This is police business. You're a civilian. Let me deal with it, OK?'

But later, when it looks like a confrontation with the Kliner boy is on the cards, he literally runs away.

> Two things happened as the Kliner kid came near. First, Finlay left in a hurry. He just strode off north without another word. Second, I heard the barbershop blinds coming down in the window behind me.

Finlay is also conflicted as a black man, of course. He knows there is a long tradition of racism among the high-ups of Margrave, but chooses to work there.

It's not altogether surprising that Finlay displays this level of conflict whereas Roscoe does not. A little conflict goes a long way, and the reader would quickly experience overwhelm if they were confronted with too many characters in a state of internal tension and confusion.

What may seem more surprising is that Finlay, a secondary character, is considerably more conflicted than the novel's main character. Reacher is faced with all sorts of challenges, but he doesn't get all eaten up about them. When he discovers that his brother has died, he does take some time to reflect, but it's not anguished indecision. It's more like tuning into his inner voice.

> And now somebody had killed him. I sat there in the back of the police Chevrolet listening to a tiny voice in my head asking me what the hell I was going to do about that.

And later.

> I leaned up against the statue in front of the station house and listened to the tiny voice inside my head saying: you're supposed to do something about that.

Contrast that with Finlay's compromised professional situation, correctly diagnosed by Reacher.

> 'You know I didn't do a damn thing. You know it wasn't me. You're just shit scared of that useless fat bastard Morrison. So I'm going to jail because you're just a spineless damn coward.'

Part of Reacher's attraction is that he is like a force of nature – a pure expression of the spirit of freedom and self-reliance, so it would be impossible for him to undergo inner conflict without disappointing us in a big way. Displacing the conflict onto Finlay does two things. Firstly, it makes Finlay a foil for Reacher's resoluteness, highlighting and magnifying it. Secondly, it gives the reader a much-appreciated hit of a literary drug that they crave: conflict.

Women

It is often said about Lee Child novels that they appeal to female readers because they represent female characters in a respectful way. There is definitely something in that idea, although it needs to be nuanced.

Let's get one thing straight, the Jack Reacher novels are not feminist fiction. There is a well-known test that is sometimes used to determine whether the genders are treated equally in a book: simply ask yourself, is there even a single episode when two women talk together about a subject that does not relate to a man in some way? By my reckoning, *Killing Floor* fails the test. No big surprise. It's no different from most other thrillers in that respect. You could also ask yourself whether there are any women among the book's 'evil' characters. That would show true even-handedness. But *Killing Floor* fails that test too.

So, are there any non-feminist representations of women in *Killing Floor*? Well, I'm pretty sure that Reacher's observation of Roscoe's breasts resting on a table top while she takes his fingerprints in Chapter 2 would not be considered particularly feminist. It does rather objectify her. But is it disrespectful to women? I don't think so. There's no leering or intimidating quality to the narrator's gaze. It's a momentary impression, and later he indicates that he's doing his best not to make Roscoe feel uncomfortable.

> I wanted to look at her nameplate over her shirt pocket. But I didn't want her to think I was looking at her breasts. I remembered them resting on the edge of the table when she took my photograph. I looked. Nice breasts. Her name was Roscoe.

Maybe some female readers would see the incident differently, but, to be honest, they're probably in a tiny minority. Gender roles and expressions of sexuality are generally pretty 'traditional' in thrillers, so it's difficult to imagine such easily offended people even picking up a Jack Reacher novel. I believe the majority of thriller readers actually enjoy the slightly unreconstructed attitudes that novels like *Killing Floor* embody. In our censorious modern age, people still like to get a fix of red-bloodedness from time to time, and it usually comes from fiction or cinema.

Even so, an author has to carefully judge what their readers consider respectful behaviour and never allow their 'good' characters to stray beyond that. The 'evil' characters are a different story. For them, leering sexual weirdness is almost a must. A little objectification of women is apparently acceptable to Lee Child's readers, especially if it's Reacher doing it. It's perfectly OK for him to talk about Roscoe's breasts and describe her in her black underwear. By contrast, outright unpleasantness towards women is not acceptable to the readers on any terms. It's such a no-no that it's used to kickstart our dislike of the Kliners, for whom creepiness seems to be genetic. Kliner senior is said to terrify his wife, and the son has been stalking Roscoe for five years.

There are six female characters other than Roscoe, by my count.

- Charlie
- Molly
- Kliner's wife
- The barber's sister
- The mother of Sherman Stoller
- The girlfriend of Sherman Stoller

Charlie has a 'crackle of toughness', we are told. This is confirmed by the fact that she takes the initiative in hiring Reacher to find her husband. It's a situation that finds a close parallel in the actions of two other women. Firstly, Molly, the informant from the Treasury, bravely goes out on a limb to help track down the killer of Joe Reacher, her lover. Secondly, the elderly sister of the barber bears witness to a cruel injustice, recounting how a member of the Teale family murdered her lover, Blind Blake. Although these female characters mainly derive their significance from male characters, (they are not so very different from the wife of Kliner in that respect), they display tremendous fortitude in keeping a lamp lit for their male partners. In this sense, they are quite unlike the weepy, passive Kliner woman. They remind me of the brave women in Latin America who, in the face of official disapproval, bear witness to the murder of their family members.

Takeaway

- The author makes sure that each character is distinct, even down to the first letter of their name.
- Within the cast of characters, there are parallels and contrasts that help to illuminate the themes of the novel.
- Characters outside Reacher's immediate circle, especially villains, are relatively two-dimensional, and when a detail is given it is usually because the information serves some aspect of plot or theme.
- There is a small group of characters close to Reacher who are characterised fairly richly. Even so, this is usually done in order to make them a better foil for Reacher's character
- Detailed, active and conflicted characters are interesting, but conflict needs to be used sparingly.
- Women in *Killing Floor* are presented respectfully but not necessarily in a way that would please feminists. Lee Child is tuned into his readers' attitudes.

4. THE STORY SPINE

… fiction started up, and we started burning brain cells on stories about
things that didn't happen to people who didn't exist. Why? The only
answer can be that humans deeply, deeply desired it.
- Lee Child, 'Jack Reacher', *The Lineup*, Otto Penzler Ed.

The most intensely discussed aspect of creative writing is, without
doubt, the structuring of stories. There are innumerable books
identifying the various stages that a narrative should go through if
it is going to be really entertaining. All of them have something that
an aspiring author can learn from, but in my experience, it's
unhelpful to obsess about them. The better way is to look at your
story idea's unique qualities and use them to spin out the thread of
your narrative. You'll gain a better understanding of this idea as you
read on.

Anatomy of a Story

There's a lot of geeky terminology that surrounds story analysis,
and usually no two people agree on the exact meaning of terms like
'story spine'. But here's my take on that particular term. If you were
to tell the story of *Killing Floor* to a friend in thirty seconds, you
would leave out all the extraneous stuff and describe the sequence
of events that most directly connects the world at the beginning of
the book with the world as it is at the end. That would be the story
spine.

    The events in your rapid retelling of the story would have

logical connections between them. For example, 'Reacher is attacked by Kliner's henchmen in New York, <u>so</u> he goes on the offensive by setting an ambush at Hubble's house.' These logical connections require the story to be told in a particular sequence. You could think of each individual event as one of the vertebrae in a real human spine. Vertebrae are all different sizes and shapes, so they could only ever occupy one particular place in the sequence of the spine. Just so with the events in a story spine. Take one out, or move it around, and the whole thing falls apart.

In addition to connecting each event with the one that comes next in the sequence, your retelling of the story would probably also provide an answer to the question 'So what?' Every story needs a so-what factor – an emotional wave that carries the main character and the reader from A to Z. It's usually associated with the big challenge confronting the main character. Consider the following story outline. A man with a broken back decides he's going to climb Mount Everest. In this case, the hero would probably be carried from the hospital bed to the summit of the mountain by a desire to prove himself. That's the so-what factor. To continue my anatomical metaphor, the so-what factor is like the spinal cord that runs the length of your spine, passing through the middle of your vertebrae.

In the best stories, the reader will know from the very start where the story spine's emotional wave is going to take the character. They should even be able to imagine the kind of scene that's going to take place when the main character overcomes their big challenge. In my example, if there were no scene at the top of Mount Everest, the reader would feel totally cheated. Naturally, the reader should have no clue whatsoever how the story is going to reach that point, but they should have a clear idea of where things are heading. The more remote and apparently unattainable the goal, the more exciting the story will be.

Let's consider how Lee Child creates a big challenge for Reacher, generating a strong emotional wave that will carry him right through to a showdown with Kliner and his cronies.

Grow a Backbone!

Allow me to state the obvious for a moment. Crime thrillers, by definition, have a story spine that is associated with some kind of criminal activity. The crime gives rise to a strong desire in the main character – usually a need to see the perpetrator brought to justice or defeated in some other way. Different crime writers find different ways of motivating their main character, but frequently they are driven by empathy or a sense of moral outrage.

Interestingly, Reacher's stance in relation to the criminal activity in Margrave is not at all straightforward. He is not immediately presented with a big, obvious challenge or inspired with strong emotions. Although those things do eventually fall into place, it's only after quite a few chapters. Let's step through Reacher's initial responses to the first murder. These are the stages by which the story spine of *Killing Floor* is set up.

Step 1: Reacher is initially a chief suspect in relation to the first murder. So, in Chapters 1 to 4, his main challenge is just to stay out of prison. Given his free-spirited approach to life, even the prospect of a weekend behind bars is a powerful motivator. He's carried along by a perfectly understandable emotional wave: the desire to get himself off the hook. There's a clear purpose to this. *Killing Floor* is the first novel in the Jack Reacher series, so it's crucial that we get to know and like the main character as soon as possible. In addition to supplying a steady flow of positive character traits in the first four chapters, Lee Child is establishing sympathy for Reacher by putting him in peril.

The story could have continued with Reacher as a suspect. He could have been thrown into prison and made to struggle against gangs and crooked warders for the rest of the novel. If he had, we would probably be anticipating a climax something like the concluding scenes of *The Shawshank Redemption* – a dramatic escape made possible by the main character's indomitable spirit. We do get a few chapters of that kind of thing in *Killing Floor*. In Chapters 5 to 8, Reacher sees off two different prison gangs when he and Hubble are locked up with dangerous lifers. But that is not going to be the long-term direction of the story. Even before the prison chapters, it was clear that the author had a rather different story spine in mind. Throughout Chapters 3 and 4, the groundwork was being laid for a new relationship between Reacher and the murder.

Step 2: Reacher's relationship to the first murder becomes that of an investigator. As early as Chapter 3, while Reacher is still in police custody, it's clear that Finlay knows, or strongly suspects that he's innocent. The two of them are talking like police partners, and their goals are gradually converging – focusing on the murder investigation. Reacher's primary motive for trying to shed light on the investigation is still, of course, a desire to avoid prison, but there are definite signs that he is genuinely engaging with the case. For example, he expresses concern that the real murderer is still on the loose while the police are wasting their time on him. He also ponders the question of who would engage in such a frenzied assault on a lifeless body. It seems like the professional curiosity of a former military policeman. Then, in chapter 4, he struggles to understand why Hubble confessed to a murder he obviously didn't commit. It's a question that shifts his attention onto the broader criminal conspiracy. Just what sort of scheme had Hubble become involved in, he wonders. Throughout the prison chapters, Reacher continues to chew on that mystery, probing Hubble for details.

When Reacher emerges from the prison and is told by Roscoe that a witness has provided him with an alibi, his chief-suspect role ends and he's free to pursue the role of an investigator. But there's a problem. Quite simply, there is absolutely no emotional wave that would convincingly carry him through such an investigation. He is a civilian with no special interest in the crime and every reason to get the hell out of town. When Roscoe picks him up outside the prison gate, he is still thinking about the case like an investigator, noting how suspicious it is that the report on his fingerprints came back quickly. But this is not enough to motivate him to stay in Margrave and see the case through. He plans to treat Roscoe to lunch and leave.

Step 3: A second transition in Reacher's relationship to the murder takes place. In Chapter 9, Reacher discovers that the victim of the first murder was his brother. The challenge of cracking the criminal conspiracy suddenly has a powerful emotional wave behind it: the desire to take vengeance and complete Joe's investigation. That is more than capable of carrying him (and us) through to the bitter end of a brutal investigation.

This point in the story – just under one third of the way into the book – is when Lee Child finally deposits us at the start of his story spine. It has been a longish journey, but worth it from a dramatic perspective. In his roles as chief suspect and investigator, Reacher revealed a whole load of attractive characteristics: everything from Sherlock-Holmes-like deductive skills to a positive attitude to women. The purpose was to make us fall in love with him, and it was successful. The result is that, when we do hear about the death of his brother, we feel for him. We are carried along by his desire for revenge and we feel confident that his personal qualities will make it an adventure worth sharing. You could think of the first third of the novel as the charging of a battery, and the remaining two thirds as the discharge.

Plot Points

The story spine establishes itself with a single shocking event: the identification of the first murder victim as none other than Reacher's brother. Although Joe was briefly mentioned near the start of the novel, it is a bolt from the blue when he actually turns up – lying on a mortuary slab. The impact of the revelation is all the greater because it occurs at the end of a chapter. This kind of moment is often referred to as a twist. We're all familiar with the concept, but perhaps you've never paused to define it. A twist is a revelation that comes out of the blue, forcing the characters and the reader to adopt a new perspective. Reacher's perspective clearly does change at this point. The experience forces him to reconsider his plans to leave town.

But the most important thing about this highly dramatic moment is that it affects Reacher's long-term goals and actions. In fact, it crystallises the big challenge that will see him through to the end of the book: the need to take revenge on the killers and complete Joe's mission. That makes it not just a twist, but also a plot point. A plot point is any moment when the main character's struggle with their biggest challenge is affected either negatively or positively – knocked back or helped in some way. All plot points are twists, but not all twists are plot points. Thriller stories are usually scattered with twists, but most of them only relate to the main character's smaller challenges, not the big challenge that stays with them throughout the book.

Lee Child's account of Joe's identification displays several features that are typical of the way plot points are handled in *Killing Floor*. Immediately after the revelation, Reacher engages in a long reflection, dwelling on the history that he shares with his brother, and the nature of their relationship. He begins by comparing the death to a crevasse opening under his feet. It gives us an impression of a powerful grief that doesn't resort to emotional displays.

> ONCE I SAW A NAVY FILM ABOUT EXPEDITIONS IN THE FROZEN arctic. You could be walking over a solid glacier. Suddenly the ice would heave and shatter. Some kind of unimaginable stresses in the floes. A whole new geography would be forced up. Massive escarpments where it had been flat. Huge ravines behind you. A new lake in front of you. The world all changed in a second. That's how I felt. I sat there rigid with shock on the counter between the fax machine and the computer terminal and felt like an Arctic guy whose whole world changes in a single step.

The reflection ends, around eight hundred words later, with a call to action.

> I sat there in the back of the police Chevrolet listening to a tiny voice in my head asking me what the hell I was going to do about that.

His mind moves on quickly. Later in the same chapter he is reflecting on the means that will be required to do something about Joe's death. His conclusion is that the forces of law and order cannot be relied on.

> I just shrugged. I felt like I wanted to keep some of the cards pretty close to my chest. If I was going to have to squeeze Hubble for something he wasn't very happy to talk about, then I wanted to do it in private. I didn't particularly want Finlay watching over my shoulder while I was doing it. He might think I was squeezing too hard. And I definitely didn't want to have to watch anything over Finlay's shoulder. I didn't want to leave the squeezing to him. I might think he wasn't squeezing hard enough.

Now we not only have a sense of Reacher's mission and the emotions that will see him through to the end, but also a sense of the rulebook that will apply for the rest of the story.

This plot point sets the pattern for those that follow. They tend to occur at the ends of chapters. After each one, the author takes time to help the reader unpack the significance of what has just happened, usually with a longish reflection. In the course of that reflection, the author provides a metaphor that deepens our insight into the event (in the current plot point it is the image of a

66

crevasse). The author also makes a point of clarifying exactly how Reacher's mission has been hindered or advanced. This is reinforced by a strong emotional response from the characters, either negative or positive.

Let's consider some other plot points in *Killing Floor.*

The next one in sequence is probably the moment in Chapter 15 when Reacher realises that Roscoe's house has been invaded. It is an unforeseen event that occurs at the end of a chapter to emphasise its importance. The significance of the episode for Reacher is made clear: he and Roscoe are at considerable personal risk if they continue to rattle Kliner's cage. In the previous chapter, Reacher had been threatening the prison warder, Spivey, trying to find out who else was involved in the criminal conspiracy. Now, he knows that he can expect a rough ride if he persists with the mission of taking revenge on Joe's murderers. These issues are patiently unpacked in a relatively static phase at the start of Chapter 16. Reacher is angry, but the emotional fallout for Roscoe is even greater.

> I saw her go pale. She shuddered. The defenses crashed down. She pressed herself into the corner by the door. Tried to flatten herself onto the wall. Stared into space like she was seeing all the nameless horrors. Started crying like her heart was broken. I stepped over and held her tight. Pressed her against me and held her as she cried out the fear and the tension. She cried for a long time. She felt hot and weak. My shirt was soaked with her tears.

It is important that the emotional fallout from a plot point is entirely believable. In this case, we can see that Lee Child has taken steps to ensure just that. The Morrison murder, in Chapter 11, planted in readers' minds the appalling savagery of the men in white overalls. And now it is paid off.

> She'd seen the Morrison corpses. I hadn't. Finlay had sketched in the details for me. That was bad enough. He'd been there. He'd been shaken by the whole thing. Roscoe had been there too. She'd seen exactly what somebody wanted to do to the two of us.

Setting us up with advance knowledge of the Morrison murder lets us share Roscoe's huge shock reaction when, just a few chapters later, her home is found to have been invaded by the same overall-clad visitors.

Lee Child further magnifies the importance of the plot point by dropping in a metaphor. Reacher compares the psychological effect of the incident to the opening of a door.

> They had pushed open the forbidden door. They had made a second fatal mistake. Now they were dead men. I was going to hunt them down and smile at them as they died. Because to attack me was a second attack on Joe. He was no longer here to stand up for me. It was a second challenge. A second humiliation. This wasn't about self-defense. This was about honoring Joe's memory.

The image communicates the significance of the event for Reacher's mission. It has pushed his desire for revenge to a new level.

The next plot point is Molly's death in Chapter 20. All the same key characteristics apply. It takes place at the end of a chapter for dramatic effect and it is followed by a period of solemn reflection. As part of the reflection, Reacher once again resorts to a metaphor in an attempt to show how important the episode is. He compares his state of mind to a diamond.

> Pressure turns coal into diamonds. Pressure does things. It was doing things to me. I was angry and I was short of time. In my mind I was seeing Molly coming out of that jetway. Striding out, determined to find Joe's brother and help him. Smiling a wide smile of triumph. Holding up a briefcase of files she shouldn't have copied. Risking a lot. For me. For Joe. That image in my mind was building up like massive pressure on some old geological seam. I had to decide how to use that pressure. I had to decide whether it was going to crush me or turn me into a diamond.

The metaphor makes the consequences for Reacher's personal mission very clear. He must become harder and more resolved than ever.

Finlay's reaction to Molly's death conveys the intensity of the emotional fallout.

> We were leaning on the front fender of Roscoe's car in the airport short-term lot. Stunned and silent. Wednesday afternoon, nearly three o'clock. I had hold of Finlay's arm. He had wanted to stay

inside and get involved. He had said it was his duty. I had screamed at him that we didn't have time. I had dragged him out of the terminal by force. I had marched him straight to the car, because I knew what we did in the next few moments was going to make the difference between winning and losing.

...

She and I drove down together in her car. Finlay was in front of us all the way. She and I didn't speak a single word. But Finlay was talking to himself through the whole trip. He was shouting and cursing. I could see his head jerking back and forth in his car. Cursing and shouting and yelling at his windshield.

Lee Child also flags up the fact that Molly's death has changed the landscape of the investigation, since her leaked Treasury documents have been stolen. This makes the struggle against Kliner even more challenging. The one possible way out is clarified in a brief passage of dialogue straight after the killing.

'We've got to go get Gray's file,' I said. 'It's the next best thing.'
Finlay shrugged. Gave up the struggle.
'It's all we got,' he said.
Roscoe nodded.
'Let's go,' she said.

The final plot point is the raid on Kliner's warehouse. In the build-up to this moment, there are many other dramatic occurrences – for example the finding of Gray's case notes at the barber's shop, or the revelation that Picard is on Kliner's team – but these are not given the lighthouse-like status of plot points. There are no extended reflections after they occur, no metaphors that emphasise the power of the events, no emotional overspill from the characters and no careful unpacking of the effect on Reacher's mission. As the story becomes more intense towards the end, it is only to be expected that there will be shocking twists, but shock alone does not make a plot point. The raid's status as the climactic plot point of the entire novel is confirmed by the tumultuous aftermath. The emotional overspill is huge.

We laughed and hugged. We danced and laughed and slapped each other's backs. We swung the children up in the air and hugged them and kissed them. Hubble hugged me and pounded me on the back. Charlie hugged me and kissed me. I lifted

Roscoe off her feet and kissed her long and hard. On and on. She wrapped her legs around my waist and locked her arms behind my head. We kissed like we would die if we stopped.

This riotous joy signals the magnitude of the victory over Kliner, as does the impressiveness of the inferno in the warehouse, which Lee Child turns into a metaphor for Reacher's victory over greed and abuse of authority.

> 'This is the best part,' she said. 'Finlay says when the roof blew off the warehouse last night, the sudden updraft of air blew the money all over the place. Remember those burning pieces that kept landing on us? There are millions of dollar bills all over the place. Miles around. The wind blew them everywhere, in the fields, all over the highway. Most of them are partially burned, of course, but some of them aren't. Soon as the sun came up, thousands of people came out of nowhere, swarming around all over the place, picking all the money up.'

The effect of the plot point spreads over into the next chapter – the final chapter of the novel. There, we see that Margrave is making a new start. It is shown, in detail, how the town has been redeemed of every ill that afflicted it.

> 'What are you going to do?' I asked her.
> She looked at me like it was an odd question.
> 'Work my butt off, I guess,' she said. 'There's going to be a lot to do. We're going to have to rebuild this whole town. Maybe we can make something better out of it, create something worthwhile. And I can play a big part in it. I'll move up the totem pole a couple of notches. I'm really excited. I'm looking forward to it. This is my town and I'm going to be really involved in it. Maybe I'll get on the town board. Maybe I'll even run for mayor. That would be a hell of a thing, wouldn't it? After all these years, a Roscoe for mayor, instead of a Teale?'
> I looked at her. It was a great answer, but it was the wrong answer. Wrong for me.

This clearly signals the end of the story spine. The mission has been accomplished, and Reacher can now move on.

Well-Known Plot Outlines

Many writers about writing have tried to define the arrangement of plot points that makes for a really effective story. I want to take two of the most influential outlines and show how the story of *Killing Floor* might fit into them. Do make sure you buy and read the original books. I have only provided minimal summaries of their ideas here, and they are both well worth having on your shelf.

First up is Blake Snyder's book *Save the Cat*. It describes a three-act structure, and is principally intended for writers creating Hollywood-type screenplays. It also works well for novels, though.

	Save the Cat	*Killing Floor* (order differs from novel)
ACT ONE	Opening image	• Reacher has just made a long rainy walk into town when he is arrested.
	Theme stated	• 'What is Pluribus?' • 'I thought I'd come and look for Blind Blake.'
	Set-up	• Reacher is totally in control, observing the technique of the arresting officers and getting the better of Finlay in the interrogation. • 'My name is Jack Reacher. No middle name. No address.' • Description of the crime by Finlay.
	Catalyst	• Hubble confesses to a murder he didn't commit.
	Debate	• In prison, Reacher tries to find out why Hubble confessed to the murder but fails. • Having exonerated himself

71

		with an alibi, Reacher wants to leave town as soon as possible.
	Break into two	• Reacher finds out that the murder victim was his brother.
ACT TWO	B story	• Reacher has sex with Roscoe.
	Fun and games	• Hubble goes missing.
		• Reacher is followed by the Kliner boy and the Hispanic henchmen.
		• Reacher kills the Hispanic henchmen.
		• Reacher makes several visits to the pathologist.
		• Morrison and his wife are murdered horribly.
		• Joe's car is found.
		• Joe's accommodation is found, although the Hispanic henchmen have beaten them to it.
		• Reacher salvages a clue from Joe's luggage.
		• Reacher carries out surveillance at the Kliner warehouse and tails a truck.
		• Reacher threatens the crooked prison warder, Spivey, trying to get information from him.
	Midpoint	• Roscoe's home is invaded by a team of sadistic killers.

Bad guys close in	• Joe's academic contacts are being killed, but Reacher manages to protect one of them.
	• Molly is killed.
	• Reacher sets an ambush at the Hubble house and kills the Kliner boy.
All is lost	• Picard turns out to be part of Kliner's gang.
Dark night of the soul	• Reacher must do the impossible: find Hubble to save Roscoe and Charlie.
Break into three	• Having located Hubble and rescued Finlay, Reacher and his allies go to the barber's shop to plan the final assault.

| **ACT THREE** | Finale | • The raid on the Kliner warehouse. |
| | Final image | • Reacher gets on a bus and leaves town. |

My second plot outline comes from *The Writer's Journey* by Christopher Vogler. It is adapted from an outline developed by Joseph Campbell, the great scholar of mythology. Vogler's influential analysis, which is often referred to as the hero's journey, distils the underlying structures of myths and legends from around the world. It describes plot in terms of a quest and return.

| | *The Writer's Journey* | *Killing Floor* (order differs from novel) |
| **ORDINARY WORLD** | Ordinary world | • At the start of the novel, Reacher is enjoying a meal |

in a diner.

	Call to adventure	• Reacher is accused of murder but exonerated.
		• Hubble confesses to the murder even though he could not have committed it.
	Refusal of the call	• After his release from prison, Reacher decides to leave Margrave.
	Meeting the mentor	• Reacher visits the barber and hears about the murder of Blind Blake.
SPECIAL WORLD	Crossing the threshold	• Reacher realises that the murder victim was his brother.
	Tests, allies, enemies	• Finlay starts to treat Reacher as an ally.
		• Hubble goes missing.
		• Reacher is followed by the Kliner boy and the Hispanic henchmen.
		• Reacher befriends the barbers and hears about the death of Blind Blake.
		• Reacher kills the Hispanic henchmen.
		• Reacher makes several visits to the pathologist.
		• Morrison and his wife are murdered horribly.
		• Joe's car is found.
		• Joe's accommodation is found, although the Hispanic henchmen have

beaten them to it.

- Reacher salvages a clue from Joe's luggage.
- Reacher threatens the crooked prison warder, Spivey, trying to get information from him.
- Roscoe's home is invaded by a team of sadistic killers.
- Joe's academic contacts are being killed, but Reacher manages to protect one of them.
- Molly is killed.

Approaching the cave	•	Reacher carries out surveillance at the Kliner warehouse and tails a truck.
Ordeal, death and rebirth	•	Reacher sets an ambush at the Hubble house and kills the Kliner boy, drowning him in a pool.
Reward – seizing the sword	•	In the barber shop, before the assault on Kliner's warehouse, Reacher hears the full story of how a Teale killed Blind Blake.
The road back	•	Reacher locates Hubble.
	•	Together, they rescue Finlay.
	•	They raid the warehouse and kill the conspirators.
ORDINARY WORLD	Resurrection	• Reacher prepares to hit the road again.
	Return with elixir	• Margrave makes a new start.

As you can see, neither of the schemes fits *Killing Floor* perfectly. For example, *Save the Cat* has far too clean a division between 'fun and games' and the stage after the midpoint when the 'bad guys close in'. Likewise, *The Writer's Journey* talks about a single, climactic death-and-rebirth ordeal, after which the hero is heading for home, even though there may be more tests to come. In *Killing Floor*, the drowning of the Kliner boy in a swimming pool fits the description of a death and rebirth ordeal, but the climax of the story is still some way off.

Nevertheless, there are important insights that you can gain from both outlines.

Save the Cat demonstrates the importance of theme. The theme needs to be stated at some point near the beginning of the first act, even if it's cloaked in mystery. In *Killing Floor*, the word 'pluribus' is a major statement of theme. Finlay asks Reacher about it during the interrogation, but he is as mystified as us about its significance. All Reacher can come up with is the Latin motto shown on American bank notes: 'E pluribus unum'. The literal meaning of the motto is 'Out of many, one', and this definition resonates with a key theme of *Killing Floor*: the tension between individual freedom and responsibility. This theme emerges gradually in the course of the book, but a particularly strong light is thrown on it by the plot points at act transitions. For example, when Reacher realises that his brother, whom he has not seen in years, is dead, he regrets the loss of their early closeness and commits himself to revenge.

The Writer's Journey provides a good insight into the nature of a hero. Truly heroic characters don't simply achieve a selfish goal, they redeem their fictional world in some way. For Reacher, it is not enough to take revenge on his brother's killer, he must also rid Margrave, and in fact the whole of the fictional world, of a grave moral ill: the corrupt and amoral rule of a wealthy elite. The huge conflagration that burns up the fake currency after the raid on the warehouse is the ultimate sign that Reacher the hero has redeemed society from enslavement to the likes of Kliner. In the final chapter, Roscoe even thinks about standing for mayor.

Takeaway

- Every story needs a spine. This is not just the sequence of events, it is also the main character's biggest challenge and the wave of emotion that gets him through it.
- Lee Child takes his time to set up the story spine. The crime is reported at the beginning of the novel, but nearly a third of the novel passes before Reacher is given a strong motivation to move against the criminals. In the meantime, his likeability is established by putting him in peril.
- *Killing Floor* contains a number of plot points.
- They are unexpected events.
- They advance or hinder Reacher's biggest challenge: revenge.
- They prompt a period of sombre reflection from Reacher, often incorporating a vivid metaphor.
- *Save the Cat* Illustrates the importance of theme. In *Killing Floor*, the plot points act as lighthouses that illuminate theme.
- *The Writer's Journey* helps us to understand the nature of a hero. Reacher fits the bill because he redeems the fictional world from moral ills while fulfilling his personal mission.

5. QUESTIONS QUESTIONS

> Waiting is a skill like anything else.
> - Lee Child, *Killing Floor*

Lee Child does a lot of public Q&A sessions, and they make fascinating viewing. He's a very entertaining guy with great life stories to tell, and he often comes up with useful insights into his creative process. In almost every discussion that I've seen, either live or on YouTube, he covers the subject of suspense. How is it created and sustained over a four-hundred-page novel? His answer is always the same: ask questions that the reader wants answers to, keep asking them, but don't provide the reader with an answer immediately. It's only logical really. The word 'suspense' means, of course, suspending or putting something off.

It's a powerful and deceptively simple technique. It creates a nagging sense of incompleteness and desire for an answer. As you read, you may not even be aware of the source of that vague anxiety, but the net result is that you keep turning the pages, hoping that your itch is going to be scratched.

Structured Suspense
Different novels take radically different approaches to the process of raising and answering questions. Some are highly structured, explaining in detail the logic and methods of an investigative process. In others, there is a sense of mystery about how and why the story's questions arise or get solved. This is probably the single

most important decision when writing a crime thriller. It will determine the shape and feel of the battle between good and evil. How does evil manifest itself? Brazenly, or does is it have to be dragged into the light? And what is it that gives your hero the edge? A methodical approach? Superior powers of reason? Team work? Luck?

The Ministry of Fear, by Graham Greene is a masterful example of a novel that creates a sense of mystery around the raising and answering of questions. It's difficult to tell whether the main character is a paranoiac or a hunted man. He has, after all, just come out of a mental hospital. So, is he imagining everything or are the questions he raises entirely valid? Some of the Martin Beck novels by Maj Sjöwall and Per Wahloo are similarly disorienting, but for different reasons. Often, Beck solves a case simply by casting his net wide to see what turns up, or even by sheer good luck.

Other authors take their investigator on a linear journey from one question to another, until finally they run out of questions. Ed McBain's 87th Precinct novels tend to be like that. Detective Steve Carella's secret weapon is his persistence.

In *Killing Floor*, the mystery is much more structured. There is a big question, several middling questions and lots of small questions. The investigation is like a machine that takes bites out of the bigger questions, chewing them up to produce smaller questions. The author keeps the biggest question unresolved for most of the novel, while the middling questions hang around for only a portion of it. The small questions are usually resolved in one or two chapters.

The Big Question: Who, How, Why

In many crime thrillers, the suspense is structured around one or more of the following big questions.

- Who did it?
- How did they do it?
- Why did they do it?

Stories structured around the first of these questions are clearly very common – so common that they represent a separate genre, with the label 'whodunnit'. In my view, *Killing Floor* is not part of the whodunnit genre. How could it be, given that the identity of the main conspirators is an open secret? From Chapter 9, when Reacher gets released from prison and starts interacting with the people of Margrave, we see and hear how evil the Kliners and Mayor Teale are. In fact, they're such obvious villains that it's very clear they are going to turn out to be responsible for the series of murders.

Killing Floor can't be a howdunnit either. Thanks to Reacher's Sherlock-Holmes-like analytical skills, we find out as early as Chapter 3 how the murder was carried out. There were three people involved, each of whom played a different role. No mystery there.

But what we don't know, is why the criminals did it – what kind of conspiracy required the murder of four people. From the reader's perspective, *Killing Floor* is clearly a whydunnit.

I say 'from the reader's perspective' for a good reason. It's because, from Jack Reacher's perspective, the events of the novel look rather different. As far as he's concerned, he's in a 'whodunnit'. He's intent on discovering the identity of the murderers – initially because he wants to avoid having the murder pinned on him, but subsequently because he wants to take revenge on his brother's killer and complete his investigation. He clearly and succinctly summarises his mission in Chapter 10.

> What was I going to do about Joe? My answer came very easily. I knew it would. I knew it had been waiting there since I first stood next to Joe's broken body in the morgue. It was a very simple answer. I was going to stand up for him. I was going to finish his business. Whatever it was. Whatever it took.

Reacher stays in whodunnit mode for around twenty chapters, until a photo emerges of Hubble and Stoller's van at the Kliner warehouse. That finally confirms Kliner's involvement in the conspiracy. But for the entirety of those twenty chapters – more than half the novel – the reader is well aware whodunnit, and has to watch as Reacher struggles to catch up. His 'whodunnit' investigations mostly coincide with and satisfy the reader's whydunnit interests, but It's an odd state of disconnect between us and the hero of the novel, and as such it demands explanation.

You can begin to understand why Lee Child keeps his hero

in the dark about the identity of the murderers, while making it obvious to the reader, if you ask yourself one simple question: would you read a novel in which the hero knew the identity of the killer and was simply trying to work out why he did it? I'm guessing the answer is 'probably not'. Whydunnit situations are inherently undramatic.

Whodunnits, by contrast, are inherently dramatic. It stands to reason that a hidden killer will be much more frightening than an enemy who's out in the open. There's the danger that they might kill again without warning, or even turn on the people pursuing them. Also, if a killer is hidden, it's often the case that their violent acts take place off stage, so to speak. You don't get to witness their savagery directly, and the anticipation is spine tingling as you imagine what it would look like. Finally, there is also something primitively satisfying about the hunt aspect of a whodunnit plot. Pursuing the quarry through a dense forest and finally digging it out of its lair is something that human beings relate to on a deep level.

In *Killing Floor*, Reacher's revenge mission brings some of those exciting whodunnit characteristics to the action, even though we are pretty sure of the identities of the bad guys. We find ourselves empathising with the huge emotional charge that drives Reacher to identify his brother's killers, and we enjoy anticipating a final scene in which they get their come-uppance. That sense of drama is the chief reason why Lee Child keeps Reacher focused on a whodunnit mission for most of the novel.

But let's not be too critical of whydunnits. They may be less enthralling, but they do have their uses. If an author wants to advocate for an ideological viewpoint, they'll often resort to a whydunnit storyline. Let's look at a particularly successful example of a whydunnit to get a better understanding of how that works.

I'm sure you're familiar with the plot outline of the classic cop movie *Dirty Harry*. A killer has been terrorising the city of San Francisco with ransom demands and murders targeted at specific social groups. He's brought down by maverick cop, Harry Callaghan, while the city's liberal authorities do their best to get in the way. The killer, Scorpio, is identified at around the halfway mark – after the minimum of investigative effort – and, from that point on, our attention is constantly drawn to the character's countercultural appearance and personality traits. The conclusion is difficult to avoid: Scorpio kills because he is, in the eyes of Callaghan, a degenerate hippie – the kind of person who imprisons naked girls underground, takes masochistic pleasure in having himself beaten up and – worst of all – has long hair.

Killing Floor has a rather different set of bad guys. Their willingness to kill is associated with their wealth and power rather than their countercultural values, but the process of demonising a particular type of person is similar to that in *Dirty Harry*. Teale and the Kliners kill – we are meant to conclude – because they are the kind of people whose relatives policed segregation with a silver-topped cane, who terrify their wives, who drive vulgar cars and who brag about owning the whole town.

Although the politics of *Dirty Harry* and the novels of Lee Child are more or less opposite, preachiness is a criticism levelled at both of them from time to time. Both provide easy answers to somewhat leading 'why' questions. In the case of *Dirty Harry*, it is 'Why do people get killed in the global capital of the counterculture, where criminals have more rights than their victims?' In *Killing Floor*, it is 'Why do people get killed in a small southern town ruled by racist plutocrats?' The answers are framed by the questions in a rather manipulative way. Nevertheless, a little preachiness seems to go a long way in crime fiction. If you hit the right political notes as a socially engaged crime novelist, you can tap into popular sentiment and enjoy cult success. The vogue for Scandinavian fiction that comments on the evils of capitalism is proof of that.

To keep readers turning the pages (or cinema-goers in their seats) whydunnit stories often compensate for their relative lack of drama by providing some other kind of hook. In both *Dirty Harry* and *Killing Floor*, the personality of the main character is a major factor in keeping you glued to the story. Jack Reacher and Harry Callaghan are both ineffably cool, and millions of people have enjoyed spending hours in their company. And when you're with a guy who delivers lines like Callaghan, or who lives by a code of freedom like Reacher, who cares too much about the drama level, eh?

The Big Question: Hints and Clues

Whether a novel revolves around a whydunnit, a whodunnit or a howdunnit question, it is a major challenge to keep that question fresh in the reader's mind from one end of the story to the other. In a complex plot, one can easily lose a sense of context. The answer is to keep producing vivid reminders. You could call these reminders 'clues', since they are often details that hint obscurely at an answer to a big investigative challenge. As such, they act as drivers for investigative activity, reappearing again and again as the case progresses, but not getting resolved until nearly the end of the novel.

In *Killing Floor*, the most obvious detail of this kind is the word 'pluribus'. It's first mentioned by Finlay as he interrogates Reacher in Chapter 2. He's quoting from a piece of paper that was hidden in the clothing of the first murder victim. Reacher immediately makes a connection between 'pluribus' and money – he knows all about the motto on US bank notes. Throughout the novel, the word continues to make occasional appearances, as Reacher questions individuals who may know something about the murders. But no one who hears it is able to clarify what it means. In Chapter 7, Hubble refuses to tell Reacher why he was shocked half to death on hearing the word 'Pluribus' from Finlay. In Chapter 18, Stoller's girlfriend has no idea what it means. In Chapter 20, the sentence 'E unum pluribus' is reconstructed from a second piece of paper found in Joe's luggage, but Reacher and we are none the wiser about the connection to the murders. In fact, the reversal of the standard American motto makes the clue even more puzzling. Only in Chapter 27 does Reacher finally connect Joe's anti-counterfeiting work with the word 'pluribus' and understand why his brother was murdered.

> ... by the time I had finished, I knew exactly how they were getting their paper. I knew exactly where they were getting it from. I knew what had been in those air conditioner boxes last year. I didn't need to go up to Atlanta and look. I knew. I knew what Kliner was stockpiling at his warehouse. I knew what all those trucks were bringing in every day. I knew what Joe's heading had meant. E Unum Pluribus. I knew why he'd chosen that reversed motto. I knew everything, with twenty-four hours still to go. The whole thing, from beginning to end. From top to bottom. From the inside out. And it was one hell of a clever operation. Old Professor Kelstein had said the paper was unobtainable. But Kliner had proved him wrong. Kliner had found a way of obtaining it. A very simple way.

Some of the details that Lee Child uses to remind us about the novel's big question are less 'clue-like'. By that, I mean they don't give rise to any investigative activity. In fact, the novel's characters remain almost unaware of them. It seems they are only intended to give the reader a vague sense of what may lie behind the murders.

For example, in Chapter 9, the extreme neatness of Margrave is noted at length.

> ... it was the most immaculate town I had ever seen. It was amazing. Every single building was either brand-new or recently refurbished. The roads were smooth as glass, and the sidewalks were flat and clean. No potholes, no cracks, no heave. The little offices and stores looked like they got repainted every week. The lawns and the plantings and the trees were clipped to perfection. The bronze statue of old Caspar Teale looked like somebody licked it clean every morning. The paint on the church was so bright it hurt my eyes. Flags flew everywhere, sparkling white and glowing red and blue in the sun. The whole place was so tidy it could make you nervous to walk around in case you left a dirty footprint somewhere.

Later, we will look back and realise that this creepy tidiness is all part of a money laundering exercise that involves pumping cash into local businesses, but for now it's just an eerie phenomenon. In the same chapter, Reacher briefly observes that he couldn't get change in the convenience store as they didn't have any dollar bills. It's a tiny detail, but, ironically, it stands out precisely because of its apparent irrelevance. Nothing is really irrelevant in a tightly written thriller like *Killing Floor*, so its unexplained presence makes our antennae twitch. For now, we have no reason to link it to criminal activity, but it keeps the issue of money in our minds.

Clues and hints like these keep the big question in our minds, giving us a vague idea of what may lie behind the murders. But the question is not fully answered until more than three-quarters of the way through the novel. As Lee Child has pointed out on many occasions, the longer you deny the reader's desire for an answer, the greater the desire becomes. I agree, but it's only half the truth. There's always a danger of readers succumbing to indifference if their curiosity is thwarted over and over again. To sustain the reader's interest, it's important to give them some minor revelations now and again. That's why, in *Killing Floor*, an array of middling-sized questions starts to emerge soon after the big question.

Middling Questions

While the tantalising mystery of the word 'pluribus' hovers over their heads, Reacher, Finlay and Roscoe tackle a number of more manageable issues. These overlap with one another considerably. Sometimes they are split up between the three of them, and sometimes Reacher moves between different issues.

The five most prominent middling-sized issues are as follows.

- What was Hubble's role in the conspiracy?
- Why was Joe Reacher in Margrave?
- What is the significance of the Sunday deadline?
- How are they getting paper for the counterfeiting?
- Who is the tenth man?

Hubble's role in the conspiracy is the most long-lasting of these questions, and therefore the one that generates most suspense. That is helped by the fact that Hubble goes missing in Chapter 9 and doesn't reappear until Chapter 30. The shortest-lived question is the one that relates to the identity of the tenth man. It occurs to Reacher towards the end of Chapter 28, and is answered almost immediately when Picard appears with a gun. Although these questions are both pieces in the puzzle of the investigation, they have very different life cycles. One long and suspenseful, one short and shocking. This difference is part of a steady ramping up of the pressure on the investigators. The questions that Reacher and the others concern themselves with initially are difficult to crack, but don't cause too many headaches while they're hanging around. But by the end of the novel, questions are arising and then blowing up in Reacher's face almost immediately.

There's an important technique that gives an extra boost to the novel's drama level as it ramps up in this way. That question about the tenth man, which arises late in the story and quickly becomes too hot to handle, is closely aligned with the story spine. As I'm sure you recall, Reacher's revenge mission is the emotional wave that drives him and us through to the end of the story – in other words, the story spine. Well, that emotional wave is what crashes into the end of the novel and produces the question 'Who is the tenth conspirator?' For one thing, the question seems to occur to Reacher in connection with thoughts of revenge.

> 'We only need to ID one more,' I said. 'I sniffed out four more last night. There's only the tenth guy we don't know.'

By 'sniffed out' he means, of course, 'killed'. And by the sounds of it, he is hoping to dish out the same treatment to the tenth man.

Although the question about the tenth man is very short lived, it's basic assumption – that there are ten conspirators to take down – was set up as early as Chapter 8. We were primed with the information by Hubble in prison and Reacher even returned to it on a couple of occasions during the novel, but the author did nothing to draw attention to the number of conspirators remaining – no description of Reacher scratching out the men's names on a wall, or whatever. The information was set up, but quietly forgotten, and only a very alert reader would even remember by Chapter 28 that there was one conspirator left to find. The result is a powerful twist in the plot. Reacher raises the question about the tenth man, Picard answers it for him, and we know straightaway that we have been caught napping.

Rather like the novel's big question, the middling-sized questions are often associated with clues and hints. A particularly strange example is seen in Chapter 26. It relates to the question about the counterfeiters' source of paper, and it is best described as a 'pre-echo' of the solution. Reacher climbs out of the swimming pool at the Hubble house, having just killed the Kliner boy. He takes a piece of paper from his pocket – the scrap that was found in Joe's luggage – and finds that the ink has been washed off. In a separate incident later in the same chapter, Reacher reflects on the question of where the counterfeiters get their paper. The swimming pool incident is still fresh in our mind and hints at the answer: they get their paper by bleaching dollar bills.

This pre-echo technique needs to be handled carefully. If it's used in an unsubtle way, it can break the fictional illusion and seem patronising to the reader. Used in a subtle way, it can elicit an unconscious response in the reader's mind, making them sensitive to questions and open to potential answers.

False trails are a key part of any mystery, although they are used sparingly in Lee Child's novels. He tends to locate his red herrings at the level of these middling-sized questions. For example, in Chapter 24, we see Finlay at the wheel of a car. He is hyped up by the pace of the investigation, driving fast while not looking at the road. It's an unsettling episode. If you have a suspicious mind, like me, you will have wondered if there is more to this Finlay guy than meets the eye. Could he be a conspirator? Creating these moments of almost unconscious doubt is easy in a clue-rich environment like *Killing Floor*. Our sensitivities are raised to a level where we latch onto almost any oddity.

Small Questions

Most of the actions carried out by Reacher, Finlay and Roscoe are linked to one or another of these low-level questions, which are in turn derived from middling-sized questions and ultimately from the big whydunnit question. A typical small question is the minor mystery that arises in Chapter 4 and gets solved in Chapter 8: why did Hubble confess to the murder? Soon after Hubble's interrogation at the police precinct, Reacher discusses the issue with Finlay. Then, during the prison chapters, he presses Hubble for an explanation. None is forthcoming, but in Chapter 8, he discovers enough about the murderous conspirators to deduce the truth. Hubble simply wanted to be safe, so he got himself thrown into prison for the weekend.

Although many of the novel's small questions are raised and answered within a single episode, it's common to see Lee Child raise such a question in one scene and solve it in another, even if it's not long afterwards. The question of why Hubble confessed to the murder is an example of this two-scene-question technique. It contributes just a little more suspense, motivating the reader to turn just a few more pages. Obviously, this technique tends to slow up the storytelling, so it becomes less useful as we approach the climax of the novel.

Timing

Part of the skill of the mystery writer is to set the pace at which questions are raised and answered. You don't want the reader to be frustrated by a lack of progress. But, equally, you don't want them to be starved of suspense due to a constant flow of easy wins.

The novel's big whydunnit question first begins to establish itself in Chapter 2, when Finlay asks Reacher if the word 'pluribus' means anything to him. It's interesting that the question doesn't get raised immediately. Lee Child takes a little time to set up characters and locations first. But once it is established, the whydunnit question doesn't get resolved until Chapter 27, as we have seen. At that point, there are still seven chapters to go. Those chapters are, as it were, a final act during which the hero must act on the solution to the big question.

The middling-sized questions vary greatly in their starting points, end points and duration. The question of Hubble's whereabouts is by far the longest lived. It goes unanswered for the greater part of the novel – around twenty chapters. To keep it fresh in our minds, the author gives us a reminder every few chapters in the form of a clue or a hint. But readers won't put up with a diet of hints for ever, so a number of other middling-sized questions rise to prominence and get resolved while the Hubble question is still hanging around.

- What was Hubble's role in the conspiracy? Answered in Chapter 32 when Hubble comes clean about how and why he got into crime.
- Why was Joe Reacher in Margrave? Answered in Chapter 16 when Reacher links Joe's Treasury job to the fact that Hubble was a banker.
- What is the significance of the Sunday deadline? Answered in Chapter 21 when Gray's notes reveal that there will be a shipment on Sunday.
- How are they getting paper for the counterfeiting? Answered in Chapter 27 after Reacher's spends all night reading articles about counterfeiting.
- Who is the tenth man? Answered in Chapter 28 when Picard reveals that he is on the Kliner team.

As you can see, the middling-sized questions mostly get resolved in the second half of the story. To keep the reader motivated during the first half of the story, a steady flow of answers to smaller questions is required.

Raising questions at the right time is just as important as

answering them at the right time. In *Killing Floor*, middling sized questions are raised throughout the novel, but they tend to be isolated from one another by at least a few chapters. This presumably helps to avoid overloading the readers.

- What was Hubble's role in the conspiracy? Raised in Chapter 4 when he confesses to the murder.
- Why was Joe Reacher in Margrave? Raised in Chapter 9 when he is confirmed as the murder victim.
- What is the significance of the Sunday deadline? Raised in Chapter 7 when Hubble is being questioned by Reacher in prison.
- How are they getting paper for the counterfeiting? Raised in Chapter 25 during Reacher's discussion with Professor Kelstein.
- Who is the tenth man? Raised in Chapter 28 in the aftermath of Reacher's realisation about the counterfeiters' source of paper.

Naturally, small questions are raised throughout the novel too. Usually there is no more than a chapter or two separating the first appearance of a small question and its answer.

Closure
It is extremely important to the success of a thriller that all questions are completely answered, leaving the mystery 100% resolved.

Chapter 21 is a key moment in the plot – a kind of turning point. It's when Reacher and Roscoe finally gain access to Grays's case notes, which reveal a wealth of information about the counterfeiting conspiracy. It's followed in Chapter 22 by a rapid joining up of the dots. Finlay is our representative as he combs through the details of Reacher and Roscoe's research. Two small uncertainties are immediately questioned and explained: firstly, Hubble's involvement in the counterfeiting operations, and, secondly, the significance of the air-conditioning units transported by Kliner's trucks. Later, Reacher and Roscoe will make a couple more deductions: that Gray must have been killed by the conspirators, and that the subsidies handed out to local businesses are a form of money laundering. There's something almost obsessive about the way Chapter 22 clears up area after area of the investigation.

It happens three more times, in Chapters 27, 28 and 31.

In Chapter 27, Reacher and Roscoe go back to Stoller's parents' house, where Reacher thinks they will find evidence to support the counterfeiting theory. Every attempt is made to ensure that the resolution of the mystery seems as concrete as possible.

> I walked over and rocked one out from the wall. Took out Morrison's knife and popped the blade. Pushed the point under the sealing tape and slit the top open. Pulled up the flaps on the top and pushed the box over.
> It landed with a dusty thump on the concrete floor. An avalanche of paper money poured out.

In the same chapter, there is a question and answer session – courtesy of Finlay once again. It runs us through the logic of Reacher's deduction.

> 'OK,' he said. "You proved it to me. Tell me how you figured it.'
> I squirmed around in the big leather seat to face him.
> 'I wanted to check Joe's list,' I said. 'That punctuation thing with the Stollers' garage. But the list had gotten soaked in chlorinated water. All the writing had bleached off.'
> He glanced across.
> 'You put it together from that?' he said.
> I shook my head.
> 'I got it from the Senate report,' I said. 'There were a couple of little paragraphs. One was about an old scam in Bogotá. There was another about an operation in Lebanon years ago. They were doing the same thing, bleaching real dollar bills so they could reprint the blank paper.'

In Chapter 28, Reacher's summary of the conspiracy goes on something of a rhetorical flight, showing the counterfeiting activity in its global context.

> 'How did it start?' I said. 'It started with Eisenhower. It's his fault.'
> 'Eisenhower?' he said. 'What's he got to do with it?'
> 'He built the interstates,' I said. 'He killed Margrave. Way back,

that old county road was the only road. Everybody and everything had to pass through Margrave. The place was full of rooming houses and bars, people were passing through, spending money. Then the highways got built, and air travel got cheap, and suddenly the town died. It withered away to a dot on the map because the highway missed it by fourteen miles.'

In this passage, every attempt is being made to ensure that the resolution of the mystery seems as universal as possible. It's almost as though the world in general is being redeemed. And in case all that were not enough, Chapter 31 expounds all the ins and outs of the conspiracy once again.

It's important that the reader understands all the logic that goes into answering every single question raised in the novel, but especially the middling and big questions. If they don't, the suspense created by the questions will not be converted into satisfaction, and the reader will go away feeling a little confused or cheated. Explaining again and again in different ways is no bad thing. If possible, the answers should clarify how the fictional world has been changed at a macro level.

Takeaway

- In *Killing Floor*, the mystery element of the story is more structured than it is in many thrillers. It has three distinct layers of questions. Big questions break down into middling and then small questions.
- *Killing Floor* is a whydunnit because we know who the criminals are.
- Reacher is given a whodunnit mission because whydunnits tend to lack drama. Whodunnits have a greater emotional charge.
- Whydunnits are useful for conveying a socially or politically engaged message, although this can come across as preachy.
- Hints and clues act as periodic reminders of the big and middling-sized questions, although, sometimes, allowing the reader to forget about a question can create an opportunity for a surprise twist.
- Timing is everything in mystery writing. Introduce questions one at a time, and leave some space around

them. Wait until the second half of the plot to start answering the middling-sized questions. Keep the small questions coming throughout the story but don't separate question and answer too much.

- Make sure all the logic is thoroughly explained when you answer your questions.

6. A STEEP AND WINDING ROAD

I had to decide how to use that pressure. I had to decide whether it was
going to crush me or turn me into a diamond.
- Lee Child, *Killing Floor*

Every novel hero is the descendant of the famous pilgrim depicted
by John Bunyan in his classic of allegorical literature, *Pilgrim's
Progress*. Bunyan takes his character on a long and arduous journey
that begins in the city of Destruction and deteriorates from there.
He passes through ordeals like the Slough of Despond, and
temptations such as Vanity Fair, until finally he passes the River of
Death and reaches the Celestial City. One image sums up his
struggle more than any other.

> ... the narrow way lay right up the Hill ... the Hill is
> called Difficulty.

That's what the plot of a good thriller should be like – a mountain
of difficulties with a narrow path to the top. Readers are sadists,
and authors should be too. The tougher you can make it for your
key characters, the more entertained your readership will be. Of
course, the intention is not to destroy or thwart them, but to make
them do exceptional things. That's why a good thriller must be
designed so that it steadily escalates the action in every way
possible.

Rising Stakes

People talk a lot about the 'stakes' in thrillers, and how they constantly need to be raised, but the term is not always well understood. The word 'stake' is borrowed from gambling, where it refers to the amount of money that you put at risk. In other words, it refers to danger that is deliberately chosen. In the context of fiction, stakes can't be purely accidental or unavoidable. They don't rise when a character is picked on by others, or when they blunder into a risky situation.

The main character in a good thriller will certainly encounter threats and accidents – lots of them. In the same situation, you or I would probably run away or put it down to experience or call the police. But what we want to read about in a thriller is a character who will run out to meet the danger. This is where the concept of stakes links up with the concept of heroism. Heroes are characters who constantly rise to the challenge. When they encounter misfortune, they respond in the only way they know how: by sticking their neck way out and putting it firmly on the line.

One feisty response to danger is not enough. Thrillers need it to happen again and again. The fictional world usually responds to a hero's impertinence by hitting them with even more misfortune. But, in reply, a true hero will only double down, crying 'bring it on'. To the reader, the hero must seem like a person edging out onto a fragile branch in order to reach a particularly ripe and delicious peach. 'Are they mad?' we must think to ourselves. 'Shouldn't they just let the peach go?' But as they continue to edge out over empty space, almost magically held aloft, we must find ourselves unable to take our eyes off them.

One of the biggest challenges for a writer of thrillers is motivating the hero sufficiently – in other words, creating a situation and a set of heroic qualities that make sense of the character's decision to risk everything. Fail in this and the reader won't buy into the rising stakes. If they don't buy into the stakes then you have no excitement and ultimately no readers. Luckily there's a reliable way to overcome this problem. It involves giving the hero something that they value greatly – something that can be threatened. Once you know what that thing is, it's simply a question of putting it in jeopardy and letting your character respond.

On first impressions, there's nothing much that Jack Reacher values. That's part of his charm, but it also makes it difficult, initially, to see how he can be persuaded to raise the stakes. However, on closer inspection, it's clear that Reacher does have something very important to lose: his freedom. That's the peach he would go out on a very spindly branch for. In fact, it's the essence of his character. In the first four chapters of *Killing Floor*, Lee Child goes to a lot of trouble to make us understand that Reacher values his freedom. This is a guy whose possessions fit into a small bag, who gets off buses in the middle of nowhere on a whim, who has no middle name and no address, who calls himself a hobo, who walks places other people drive, whose mail is forwarded by his bank, and so on. In short, he is the sort of guy who would pull out all the stops to avoid being incarcerated.

And pull out all the stops he does. Unlike Hubble, he doesn't cave in to his interrogators or cringe in the corner of the cell. He reasserts his freedom of spirit. In this passage, he makes Finlay wait for information about his background.

> 'Did you specialize?' he asked. 'In the service?'
> 'General duties, initially,' I said. 'That's the system. Then I handled secret security for five years. Then the last six years, I handled something else.'
> Let him ask.
> 'What was that?' he asked.

Reacher's refusal to let the police have total control undoubtedly puts him at risk of antagonising them and losing his freedom anyway, but a true hero doesn't back down, he goes all in. Even conciliatory gestures are rejected.

> 'If I'm wrong, I'll buy you lunch on Monday,' he said. 'At Eno's place, to make up for today.'
> I shook my head again.
> 'I'm not looking for a buddy down here,' I said.

In spite of his bravado, within four chapters, Reacher has been sent to prison. What now? It's a genuine challenge for the author. The hero's branch seems to have snapped and there's a danger that the story could stall. But, have no fear. There are many other branches, and all of them are higher. Three things now happen, which combine to ensure that Reacher's stakes rise inexorably towards the climax.

Firstly, while a character lives, there is always something more that can be threatened. Reacher may have lost his freedom, but he still has his life – for now. During the prison chapters, the risks to life and limb go from bad to worse. We discover that he and Hubble have been put on the same floor as dangerous lifers. It's always good practice to thoroughly clarify the risks as a character accepts higher stakes, and that is exactly what the author does.

> We were among dangerous lifers on the third. There was no upside. The downside was extensive. We were new boys on a convict floor. We would not survive without status. We had no status. We would be challenged. We would be made to embrace our position at the absolute bottom of the pecking order. We faced an unpleasant weekend. Potentially a lethal one.

What makes this a stakes-raising situation is that Reacher has a choice how to respond. It may only be the choice of confronting danger or cringing before it, but it's still an opportunity for Reacher to show his heroic qualities. He does so – with a headbutt to a gang member's face. Afterwards, he reflects that the decision was a good one. The gamble paid off.

> I felt terrible. But not as bad as I would have felt if I hadn't done it. They'd have finished with Hubble by then and started in on me.

Now we come to the second stakes-raising technique that Lee Child makes available to his hero. In the course of events, Reacher discovers something that he barely knew he valued: an almost-forgotten attachment to family. The murder of Reacher's brother creates entirely new possibilities for pushing the hero out on a limb. The two of them may have drifted apart, but a tie of kinship and responsibility remained between them.

> Plenty of times I would run out into some new schoolyard and see a bunch of kids trying it on with the tall skinny newcomer. I'd trot over there and haul them off and bust a few heads. Then I'd go back to my own buddies and play ball or whatever we

were doing. Duty done, like a routine. It was a routine which lasted twelve years, from when I was four right up to the time Joe finally left home. Twelve years of that routine must have left faint tracks in my mind, because forever afterward I always carried a faint echo of the question: where's Joe? Once he was grown up and away, it didn't much matter where he was. But I was always aware of the faint echo of that old routine. Deep down, I was always aware I was supposed to stand up for him, if I was needed.

As the song lyric goes, you don't know what you've got till it's gone. Reacher's situation is a case in point. He rediscovers fraternal feelings, but only through the loss of his brother. Once again, he has a choice about how to respond to the feeling of vulnerability. It's a question that he voices several times.

> … what the hell was I going to do about that.

He could walk away or leave it to the police. That's probably what we, the readers, would do. But Reacher is different. Over the course of Chapter 10, a sense of conviction builds in him and emerges in a clear statement of purpose.

> It was a very simple answer. I was going to stand up for him. I was going to finish his business. Whatever it was. Whatever it took.

He knows it's going to be a high-stakes trip out onto a very dangerous-looking branch, but he embraces it anyway. The risk lies in the illegality of what he's going to do – under the noses of the police. 'Finlay,' he says, 'wouldn't sanction the kind of punishments that needed to be handed out.' Reacher's right. Margrave's head detective foresees exactly what Reacher plans to do and takes steps to prevent it.

> 'What are you going to do, Reacher?' he asked me.
> 'I'm going to think about that,' I said.
> Finlay looked straight at me. Not unfriendly, but very serious, like he was trying to communicate an order and an appeal with a single stern eye-to-eye gaze.
> 'Let me deal with this, OK? he said. 'You're going to feel pretty bad, and you're going to want to see justice done, but I don't

want any independent action going on here, OK? This is police business. You're a civilian. Let me deal with it, OK?'

Warnings from a cop make no difference to Reacher. The hero's choice will always be to run towards risk if something they value highly has been attacked.

There is an immutable law of fictional stakes: if a character says they're going to go out on a limb, the author must ensure that they do so, and preferably take steps in that direction as soon as possible. In *Killing Floor*, it's not long before Lee Child obliges. In Chapter 15, Reacher guns down two men who have been following him. He even links this to the death of his brother.

> The bullets had made quite a mess. I looked down at the two guys in the silence and thought about Joe.

The revenge mission is in motion, and the author seems to be fulfilling his contract with the reader. So far so good. But then something happens. Basically, the story doesn't deliver the major risk that we were promised. Reacher never falls foul of the law as a result of this incident or any other violent episode in his revenge mission. It was signalled to us by Finlay's warning Reacher's furtiveness, but never delivered. In addition to shooting the two henchmen, he sets an ambush at the Hubble house, and, finally, stages an assault on the Kliner warehouse. But not once before the final chapter does he get any serious heat from Finlay, Roscoe or any other cop. Sure, Reacher has to sneak around a bit at the police headquarters to avoid Teale. But that's it. He more or less kills with impunity. In the final chapter of the novel, law enforcement agencies are said to have sniffed around the events in Margrave, and Roscoe becomes disillusioned with Reacher because of the violence he dished out, but those things are just the author tidying up loose ends. So, if there is a flaw in the way Lee Child handles Reacher's stakes in *Killing Floor*, it's that he never delivers on a promised threat from the law.

And, finally, we come to the third stakes-raising technique deployed by the author. We have already seen how fresh possibilities for risk and heroism were generated when Reacher discovered a new area of vulnerability: family. In the second half of *Killing Floor*, Lee Child delivers even more surprises, but of a different kind. The novel enters a phase in which nothing is what is seems. Features of the world that previously seemed good, or at least innocuous are shown to be rotten to the core.

Chapter 22 is a particularly important moment from this point of view. During a visit to the pathologist, it's confirmed that Gray was murdered rather than dying at his own hand. Other members of the police department must be implicated. The discovery rocks the world of Roscoe in particular.

> 'I was at his funeral,' she said. 'We were all there. Chief Morrison made a speech on the lawn outside the church. So did Mayor Teale. They said he was a fine officer. They said he was Margrave's finest. But they killed him.
>
> She said it with a lot of feeling. She'd liked Margrave. Her family had toiled there for generations. She was rooted. She'd liked her job. Enjoyed the sense of contribution. But the community she'd served was rotten. It was dirty and corrupted. It wasn't a community. It was a swamp, wallowing in dirty money and blood. I sat and watched her world crumble.

Reacher pushes the revelation still further, undermining even more cherished notions. He explains that Finlay only got his job as head detective because he seemed ineffective. The police chief and mayor didn't want someone who would interfere in their conspiracy.

> 'They hire in a replacement,' she said. 'Finlay, down from Boston. A guy who is even smarter and even more stubborn than Gray was. Why the hell would they do that? If Gray was a danger to them, then Finlay would be twice as dangerous. So why did they do that? Why did they hire somebody even smarter than the last guy?'
>
> 'That's easy,' I said. 'They thought Finlay was really dumb.'

The rottenness doesn't stop at the police department, but goes out in all directions to encompass the whole of public life in Margrave. Reacher realises that every business in the town is being used to launder the money from the conspiracy.

> I had expected to feel better when I had identified the opposing players. But it wasn't what I had expected. It wasn't me against them, played out against a neutral background. The background

wasn't neutral. The background was the opposition. The whole town was in it. The whole place was bought and paid for. Nobody would be neutral.

The way Lee Child pushes the threat outward and upward as far as it will go is the key to this strategy for raising the stakes. When the entire fabric of society turns out to be against the hero, the hero will clearly have to go out on a very dramatic limb. Reacher doesn't hesitate in seizing the challenge. The next time he bumps into Teale, he shows a level of animosity that's completely new.

> 'I could tear your head off,' I said to him. 'And then I could stick it up your ratty old ass.'
> We stood and glared at each other for what seemed like a long time. Teale gripped his heavy cane like he wanted to raise it up and hit me with it. I could see his hand tightening around it and his glance darting toward my head. But in the end he just stalked out of the office and slammed the door. I reopened it a crack and peered out after him. He was picking up a phone at one of the squad room desks. He was going to call Kliner. He was going to ask him when the hell he was going to do something about me.

By goading the enemy, Reacher has effectively invited them to redouble their attacks. But, that's a price he's clearly willing to accept. After all, his mission now encompasses not just revenge but the redemption of society. As the threats facing Reacher become more general and universal in significance, his goals do too. You probably recall how, in Chapter 28, he describes the investigation in the broadest of historical perspectives.

> 'How did it start?' I said. 'It started with Eisenhower. It's his fault.'

He's now effectively redeeming American society.

Before we finish with the subject of stakes, there are a few more short points that need to be made.

1) Plot points, which were discussed in a previous chapter, play an important role in forcing step changes in Reacher's stakes. Firstly, the death of Reacher's brother propels him into a criminal netherworld. Once he is down there, he can either let the proper authorities clean things up or step outside the law and do it himself.

He chooses the latter. The second plot point, the invasion of Roscoe's home by a kill team, demonstrates that the people responsible for enforcing the law are now helpless. It puts Reacher on a war footing. Two chapters later, he is confronting the same kill team face to face. Thirdly, the death of Treasury official Molly Beth Gordon snatches away the evidence that Reacher needs. The only option is to recover Gray's case notes, a move that reveals the scale of the conspiracy Reacher is dealing with.

2) It's not just Reacher who has a lot at stake. Finlay and Roscoe have plenty to lose through their involvement with him. Initially, it's just their jobs that are on the line as they sneak around the station behind Teale's back. Later, it's their lives. Reacher breaks the news to Finlay that he can expect a visit from Morrison's killers now that he's the senior police officer in Margrave. And, of course, Roscoe has a very close brush with the same white-overall-wearing sadists. But are either of them deterred? Of course not. As close associates of the novel's hero, they share some (but not all) of his exceptional characteristics.

3) When Lee Child is setting up a situation in which a character can raise their stakes, he usually takes a moment to make it explicitly clear how they're threatened. Without a good understanding of the danger, readers may not be persuaded that a character is acting heroically by putting more at risk. They may seem foolish, or gung-ho. For example, Chapter 6 ends by crystallising the risks Reacher and Hubble are now exposed to in prison. We are encouraged to anticipate the danger and even savour it. We start to imagine the kind of heroic, stakes-raising activity that will take place as they deal with the threat. It makes us feel invested in Reacher's response to the danger when it happens.

4) As the raid on Kliner's warehouse shows, you simply can't have too much at stake when it comes to the climax of an action thriller. Not content with pushing Reacher well beyond the rule of law, Lee Child reveals that there is a risk of harming Charlie Hubble's children during the raid.

Increasing Intensity

Alongside the rising stakes, a number of other techniques are used in *Killing Floor* to create the impression of rising intensity in the action. From the opening chapters, which are mostly about getting to know the main character, the novel winds itself up to a climax that is complex and violent.

It's very noticeable that the challenges encountered by Reacher and his allies become more and more difficult and dangerous. This applies not only to the conflicts that they become embroiled in but also to the investigative tasks that they have to work through.

Let's consider the increasing intensity of the investigative tasks.

The first major piece of investigative activity that Reacher engages in is a visit to the pathologist at Finlay's invitation in Chapter 9. While there, he demonstrates his expertise as a criminal investigator, explaining that there were probably three attackers. It's rather low-key stuff, although it concludes with a savage twist: the discovery that Joe Reacher is the murder victim.

From Chapters 13 to 17, the number of lines of inquiry increases, but they are familiar policing activities: tracing a car, finding out someone's last known address, etc. Tasks are assigned to Roscoe, Finlay or Reacher and proceed simultaneously, which creates a sense of busy activity. There are lots of short interactions as they report progress to one another, so the action seems to move along quickly.

In Chapter 21, Reacher's investigative problems start to become distinctly gnarly, thanks to a complex sequence in which Reacher locates Gray's missing files. It plays out in several stages. First, Reacher and Roscoe recognise the importance of the gun box, then they need to find the key inside it, then they need to understand that the key will open something that the barbers are looking after, then the right person needs to ask the barbers for the files. It's like intricate clockwork, and it results in a big win: Gray's case notes detailing the scope of the counterfeiting conspiracy.

In the chapters that follow, the investigators try to prove or disprove Gray's theories. That involves greater danger and activities that require extreme physical stamina. In particular, Reacher carries out a military-style surveillance in Chapter 23. In Chapter 25, he draws in sources of information from outside the narrow world of Margrave – namely Professor Kelstein. The scope and difficulty of the investigation are both increasing.

Finally, in Chapter 29, Reacher is confronted with an almost unimaginably difficult task. He must find Hubble while working against the clock, with Roscoe and Charlie's lives in peril and Picard breathing down his neck. This is the novel's most intense display of investigative activity. The intensity is not just due to the difficulty of the tasks and the risks involved. There are other factors. Firstly, the solution reaches deep into Reacher's past, as he explains.

> 'How the hell did you find me?' he asked.
> I shrugged at him again.
> 'Easy,' I said. 'I've had a lot of practice. I've found a lot of guys. Spent years picking up deserters for the army.'

Secondly, the investigative challenge has elements of violence: Reacher has to rid himself of Picard and a couple of henchmen before he can complete it.

This is a good point to start considering the conflict in the novel and how it, too, increases in intensity. The first major incident occurs in Chapter 2, when Reacher has a threatening encounter from Chief Morrison. Although Morrison uses some pretty colourful words to describe the fate that could befall Reacher, but the hero is dismissive.

> … this fat police chief was a waste of space. Thin dirty hair. Sweating, despite the chilly air. The blotchy red and gray complexion of an unfit, overweight mess. Blood pressure sky-high. Arteries hard as rocks. He didn't look halfway competent.

Sure enough, the encounter peters out as Morrison explains that he's too busy to deal with the suspect himself. The novel's conflict level is starting low, just like the investigative side of the plot.

Things start to heat up a little in Chapter 6, when Reacher headbutts a prison-gang member.

> Then I cheated. Instead of counting three I headbutted him full in the face. Came off the back foot with a thrust up the legs and whipped my head forward and smashed it into his nose. It was beautifully done. The forehead is a perfect arch in all planes and very strong. The skull at the front is very thick. I have a ridge up there like concrete. The human head is very heavy. All kinds of neck muscles and back muscles balance it. It's like getting hit in the face with a bowling ball. It's always a surprise. People expect punching or kicking. A headbutt is always unexpected. It comes out of the blue.
> It must have caved his whole face in. I guess I pulped his nose and

smashed both his cheekbones. Jarred his little brain around real good. His legs crumpled and he hit the floor like a puppet with the strings cut. Like an ox in the slaughterhouse. His skull cracked on the concrete floor.

Even this incident lacks a real sense of struggle. It's such a drawn-out description, that it's almost like a slow-motion movie – an appreciation of Reacher's prowess.

In Chapter 18, Reacher kills two Hispanic henchmen who have been following him. Although he comments that ambush techniques were a part of his military training, the emotional level is higher than the previous incident. He registers the effect of discovering Spivey's body.

> … my heart was thumping harder than it should have been and a cold blast of adrenaline was shaking me up. It was the sight of Spivey lying there with his legs folded sideways that had done it. I breathed hard and got myself under control.

But Reacher's ambush at the Hubble house, in Chapter 26, is several notches further up the violence scale. It involves more preparation and more opponents. We have also been primed with information about the sadism that the opponents like to indulge in. Reacher palpably struggles. He doesn't simply shoot his enemies in the back like the Hispanic henchmen, he has to employ close-up-and-personal methods like killing with a kick to the head, and drowning.

Now we come to the final conflict: the raid on the warehouse. Picard is key to the intensity of this episode. Every time we have seen him, up to that point, his size has been commented on. And, as it turns out, he is capable of being shot with a Desert Eagle and coming back for more. He is a distant cousin of Arnold Schwarzenegger's character in *Terminator*. It's slightly surprising that Reacher doesn't dispatch his enemies in rising order of importance, since Kliner is shot before Picard, but the dramatic impact of slaying a monster last of all clearly provides maximum intensity.

The next intensity-raising technique I want to discuss is familiar from many novels and films. During the prison chapters, Lee Child introduces a time limit that will put pressure on Reacher to act quickly. Hubble mentions that there will be something important happening on the coming Sunday, and that, afterwards, the conspirators will be less vulnerable. The nature of the Sunday occurrence is not revealed, and that has the effect of increasing the reader's suspense still further. The author goes on to repeatedly remind us about the deadline. It's like a ticking clock. Reacher refers to it in Chapters 10 and 14. Then Molly uses her dying breath to warn him about it. The nature of the deadline is finally revealed in Chapter 21 when Reacher realises that the warehouse will be emptied of evidence on Sunday.

There is a clear effect of all this rising intensity on Reacher. It induces a state of sharper focus and fiercer determination. This, in itself, magnifies the reader's sense of intensity.

The early chapters are carefully calibrated to make Reacher appear entertaining and personable. Even in the stressful situation of being arrested for murder, it's his lively intelligence and flippant wit that come across. But once the investigation begins, he's launched on a new trajectory. It begins with that statement of single-minded commitment to revenge.

> It was a very simple answer. I was going to stand up for him. I was going to finish his business. Whatever it was. Whatever it took.

No sign of the flippancy now. And when Roscoe's house is invaded, his firmness of purpose is taken to a new level. He describes himself as an invincible force that will protect Roscoe at all costs.

> I wanted her to see this huge guy. A soldier for thirteen long years. A bare-knuckle killer. Icy blue eyes. I was giving it everything I had. I was willing myself to project all the invincibility, all the implacability, all the protection I felt. I was doing the hard, no-blink stare that used to shrivel up drunken marines two at a time. I wanted Roscoe to feel safe.

In Chapter 21, when Molly dies, he pushes this ruthless, ultra-focused state even further.

> I had to decide how to use that pressure. I had to decide whether it was going to crush me or turn me into a diamond.

The diamond image is a vivid metaphor that describes the perfect focus and near-indestructibility that he will need if he's going to overcome his enemies. After this point, his decision-making is strongly influenced by his military training. In Chapter 25, he concludes that a confrontation with the enemy is necessary, and he goes about setting up the ambush at the Hubble house. Interestingly, we don't see or hear any of his planning for that event – it's as though he has entered a state in which he no longer reflects out loud, but just acts instinctually. Later, in the raid on the warehouse, there is zero reflection for the benefit of the reader, only remorseless, machine-like action.

In addition to this robotic, military persona that comes over Reacher, the latter part of the novel sees a stripping down of his humanity, so that he becomes a more primitive and brutal creature. We see him stacking up bodies after the fight at the Hubble house – a predator. Then later, when he's in the clutches of Kliner, he taunts his enemy by hinting at the fate of Kliner junior. It's very primal stuff – a death struggle taking place on the most basic psychological level.

The thing that connects both the 'automaton' Reacher and the 'primitive killer' Reacher is the quality of remorselessness. In his own mind, he is a force that nothing can stop. In Chapter 29, the certainty with which he pronounces Kliner's death – to the man's face – defies the elaborate obstacles in his way.

> Kliner was sneering at me. I smiled at him. Kliner was a dead man. He was as dead as a man who has just jumped off a high building. He hadn't hit the ground yet. But he'd jumped.

The thrill of anticipation is huge as we wonder, how on earth is he going to turn this around?

There's yet another intensity-building technique in *Killing Floor* that I'd like to discuss. As the story proceeds, it's noticeable that more and more powerful emotions are expressed by a number of different characters. At the start of the novel, Reacher is calmly eating breakfast in a diner, and his emotions aren't even roused very much when he's arrested. When it becomes clear that he will be spending the weekend in prison, he shows anger, but that soon dissipates and he sets himself to getting through his incarceration by sleeping and listening to his internal personal stereo. But contrast that early calmness with the volcanic overflow of emotion in Chapter 32 – the moment of triumph over Kliner.

> We laughed and hugged. We danced and laughed and slapped each other's backs. We swung the children up in the air and hugged them and kissed them. Hubble hugged me and pounded me on the back. Charlie hugged me and kissed me. I lifted Roscoe off her feet and kissed her long and hard.

The emotional journey between those two points is managed very skilfully, as key events in the story take the characters and us to new levels of emotion. Roscoe's tearful reaction to the house invasion and Finlay's raging response to the death of Molly are good examples. Significantly, they are both plot-point episodes. Plot points are moments in a novel when emotional truth asserts itself particularly forcefully.

Lee Child executes these emotional step changes without succumbing to shrillness, which is a considerable achievement. It's partly a question of pacing the increase in the emotional level, but it's also about giving the reader a break sometimes. In Chapter 19, we are told about a night spent by Reacher and Roscoe in a hotel, including a rather humdrum breakfast.

> Breakfast came and we ate it. The whole bit. Pancakes, syrup, bacon. Lots of coffee in a thick china jug. Afterward, I lay back on the bed. Pretty soon started feeling restless. Started feeling like it had been a mistake to wait around. It felt like we weren't doing anything.

Why do we need to hear this? Partly to show us that they are waiting for calls from Molly and Picard, but also to change the texture and release some of the intensity before we get back into the investigation.

There's more than one way to paint a vivid emotional canvas in a novel. So far, we have seen emotional intensity created through descriptions of people and activity. But there are other approaches. For example, Lee Child uses an old literary trick called 'pathetic fallacy'. This is when the weather in the novel echoes human emotion. Remember the description of the storm in Chapter 25.

> I walked out to find the car. Felt a warm wind blowing out of the north. The storm was going to be a big one. I could feel the voltage building up for the lightning.

In this case, the threatening thunderstorm conveys the idea of powerful emotions, slowly gathering. In the following chapter, the storm breaks just as Reacher executes his ambush, dramatising the release of fear and pent up violence.

Another indirect technique for upping the emotional level of the novel is related to vocabulary. As the story proceeds, we hear increasingly emotive language used in the narration. In the first half of the novel, Reacher's words are quite flat and calm. Even the act of killing is described with near indifference.

> I shot them both in the back as they stood there. Two quick shots.

But in the later chapters, he even resorts to lurid similes while describing violent action.

> like a ghost from hell
> …
> like banshees

The author puts these overwrought phrases into Reacher's mouth in order to tweak the reader's emotions. The aim is to make our pulse beat faster as the novel's climax approaches.

The Pendulum

We have established that *Killing Floor* is on an upward trajectory towards higher stakes, more difficult challenges, sharper mental focus and stronger emotions. But that is not the whole picture. In a truly satisfying story, the path taken by the main characters should not simply climb the mountain side but also wind about, making a sudden drop, followed by a fresh ascent, then another drop, and so on. Always the tendency should be upward, but with periodic setbacks. Put another way, the advantage should swing back and forth between the good guys and bad guys. In a crime thriller, this principle is likely to affect both the conflict between characters and the investigative activity.

In *Killing Floor*, a typical sequence of conflict-related pendulum swings proceeds as follows. The plus and minus signs indicate advantage or disadvantage for the hero.

Chapter 1

- – Reacher is arrested.
- + Reacher patiently describes the mistakes made by the arresting officers.

Chapter 2

- – Reacher is addressed by an extremely hostile police chief called Morrison.
- + As he is interrogated, Reacher establishes a kinship with Finlay by revealing his military-police background.
- – Morrison is now claiming that he saw Reacher at the crime scene.

Chapter 3

- + Reacher's insights into the murder make an impression on Finlay.
- – Reacher learns that he's still going to prison for the weekend.

Chapter 4

- + Hubble confesses to the killing.
- – The confession is obviously false, so Reacher isn't exonerated after all.

Chapter 5

- – Reacher loses his cool as he realises there's a plausible case against him.
- + Finlay empathises. He'll buy Reacher dinner if he turns out to be innocent.
- – He ends up going to prison anyway.

Or, consider the following sequence of investigative events.

Chapter 18

- + Reacher and Roscoe track down what they think is Sherman Stoller's house.
- – The house turns out to be Stoller's parents' address.

- + They go to the actual home address of Stoller – a suspiciously plush apartment.
- - Stoller's girlfriend is asked about the word 'pluribus', but she knows nothing about it.
- + She shows them a picture of Stoller that has Hubble in the background. It was taken at Kliner's warehouse.

Chapter 19

- + Roscoe links the vehicle in the photo to a company owned by Kliner.
- - Neither Molly nor Picard are calling as expected.
- + Finlay has identified Joe Reacher's hotel accommodation.
- - They have been beaten to the room by a henchman.
- + Reacher guesses where the henchman will have disposed of Joe's luggage. In it, they find the rest of the piece of paper that was on Joe's body.

Later on in the story, the pendulum swings become more and more extreme in both directions. Firstly, the author creates a false dawn for the good guys. In Chapter 28, they are in full self-congratulation mode, having worked out what the counterfeiters are doing. They just need to go through the motions of bringing them down – or so they believe. That's when the hammer falls, and things start to favour the bad guys in a big way. There is a long run of very bad news for Reacher.

- - Picard reveals himself as one of Kliner's gang.
- - Kliner turns up with a gun and reveals that Roscoe and Charlie are in captivity.
- - Reacher is given the seemingly insurmountable task of finding Hubble.

With the unearthing of Hubble, the pendulum swings back in Reacher's direction, handing him a long sequence of victories.

- + The rescue of Finlay.
- + The revelation of the truth about Blind Blake's murder.

- + The successful raid on the police precinct.

We then enter a new phase with the warehouse raid. It's a rapid sequence of very sharp swings back and forth. The action comes down to a single nail-biting moment in which the pendulum could go either way. Will Reacher or Kliner fire first? The moment of uncertainty is strung out for as long as possible, describing the details in ultra-slow motion, and in the end Reacher triumphs. Even then, our emotions are wrung out just a little more by the resurrection of Picard – a final unexpected swing to the bad guys. But with that threat defeated, the action moves swiftly to a display of emotional release.

Takeaway

- 'Stakes' are voluntarily accepted risk. The best way to motivate the character to raise the stakes is to threaten something they hold dear.
- As the novel proceeds, Reacher's stakes are renewed. The threats and goals become bigger and more universal in significance.
- Plot points are key moments that represent a step change in both the threat and the hero's response.
- All the key characters have high stakes.
- Risks and threats are thoroughly clarified whenever the hero is about to go further out on a limb.
- At the story climax, the author piles on extra threats .
- The author also turns up the intensity dial by increasing the difficulty of challenges, by reminding the reader of a time limit, by focusing the main character's state of mind and by raising the emotional level.
- The advantage swings backwards and forwards between the good guys and the bad guys. The changes in fortune become more extreme towards the end of the story, and there is a particularly frenetic set of swings at the climax.

7. VALUES AND THEMES

'I worked thirteen years, got me nowhere. I feel like I tried it their way,
and to hell with them. Now I'm going to try it my way.'
- Lee Child, *Killing Floor*

The values that the main character lives by in a novel have a huge
influence on its popularity or unpopularity. In the modern fiction
market, many readers seem to quite like a little didactic moralising.
But there are rules that you have to abide by if you want to remain
in your readers' good books.

The Rules
Firstly, the values that characterise your main character have to be
in tune with the readers' own ideas about life. Don't expect to use
your novels as a tool for converting the world to your opinions.
Popular novelists are primarily entertainers, not politicians. If your
readers are particularly receptive to a viewpoint, you can slip it in.
But that's about all you can expect to do. Make a false ideological
step, and you can very quickly alienate people.

Some of you may conclude that the key to success is to
know your readers, research their values and write characters that
suit them. In my view, that will always come across as fake. To
some extent, an author has to be 'of the people' in order to appeal
to a mass public, but that should be a genuine feature of your
personality, not an affectation.

Secondly, when you select the values of your main

character, the prime consideration should be dramatic potential. Will a particular set of values help you give the readers a satisfying and meaningful experience? Modern readers rarely find static values entertaining. It's increasingly important that the main character, even in an action thriller, goes through a moral transformation. It doesn't have to be a personal upheaval, but it does have to be a change that enshrines some kind of moral wisdom. Even if the reader couldn't put the experience into words, the story has to leave them with a feeling that something important happened during the time that they were reading your book.

Thirdly, a word about series of novels. It's all very well to give the main character a moral journey in a standalone novel, I hear you say. But what about series? It's already a major challenge to create a character who will sustain readers' interest over a series of novels, but making them go on a moral journey in every one of those novels is surely unrealistic. After all, how much moral transformation can a character undergo from book to book without ceasing to be plausible or even familiar to the reader?

It's a fair point, and it demands a special response from the author if character consistency and moral drama are going to be kept in balance. The Jack Reacher novels are a good example of how that can be done. Lee Child goes to great lengths to make his main character synonymous with a single value: the idea of freedom. Then, in each story, he holds up a different facet of that value to the light, examining it in detail and subjecting it to challenges. Each of those challenges is potentially the source of a minor transformation in the main character's values.

Let's look at how, exactly, the author establishes Reacher's freedom ethic and brings forward various aspects of it for consideration.

Freedom

In the preceding chapter, we saw how stakes and the concept of heroism are closely bound up. A hero freely chooses risk. Often, it's in defence of something that they value highly. In the early chapters of *Killing Floor*, it's love of freedom that motivates Reacher to go out on a limb. The thought of going to prison has him so rattled that it's practically the only time he expresses a sense of defeat in the whole novel.

Now I was truly pissed off. I was going to prison for the weekend.

...

I stared at him. I was getting mad.

'No, Finlay, not OK,' I said. 'You know I didn't do a damn thing. You know it wasn't me. You're just shit scared of that useless fat bastard Morrison. So I'm going to jail because you're just a spineless damn coward.'

Finlay's interrogation in those early chapters clearly reveals Reacher's free-spirited nature. We are amused by his witty responses and uncooperative behaviour. 'Let him ask,' he says (over his shoulder to the reader) as he gives Finlay the bare minimum of information about his army career. We also hear about his odd, rootless lifestyle and unique habits. The head-stereo episode in Chapter 4 is a typical example: confined to a police cell, Reacher whiles away the time by replaying his favourite musical tracks in his head, from memory.

To drive the point home that Reacher is defined by the idea of freedom, the author creates a telling contrast between Reacher and Finlay. Reacher is the mysterious hobo, with 'No middle name. No address.' Finlay is the exact opposite: a stickler for rules and procedures. 'This guy Finlay was going to go through all the hoops with this,' comments Reacher as he realises that the head detective is going to take his time and get to the truth. The man's appearance and body language send a similar message.

FINLAY LEANED RIGHT BACK IN HIS CHAIR. HIS LONG ARMS were folded behind his head. He was a tall, elegant man. Educated in Boston. Civilized. Experienced.

As the temperamental opposite of Reacher, he highlights Reacher's freedom-loving nature.

Now skip to the end of the novel. The very last thing we hear about is Reacher getting on a bus and leaving town. He even sheds the clothes that he acquired as part of the investigation. It's almost a ritual, designed to restore him to his natural state of rootlessness.

I walked into the depot. Bought a ticket. Then I crossed the street to a cheap store and bought new clothes. Changed in their cubicle, left the filthy old fatigues in their garbage can. Then I strolled back and got on a bus for California.

It's as though freedom is an element that he emerges from at the beginning of each novel in the series, and which he returns to at the end of each final chapter. But between the covers of each of the books, Reacher's freedom is challenged and explored.

Facets of Freedom

In the pages of *Killing Floor*, two aspects of freedom are explored and challenged: individualism and anti-authoritarianism.

A strong streak of individualism runs through Reacher's personality. His quirky, self-reliant lifestyle speaks for itself. It's also extremely telling that his reason for being in Margrave in the first place is to pay homage to one of his musical heroes, Blind Blake. The blues singer seems to have been an individualistic wanderer – a man after Reacher's own heart.

> The black road blasted heat at me. Blind Blake had walked this road, maybe in the noon heat. Back when those old barbers had been boys this had been the artery reaching north to Atlanta, Chicago, jobs, hope, money.

It's a rather romantic and attractive form of individualism that we see in Reacher much of the time – all about singing the blues and living life on your own terms. But we also need to acknowledge a different, and perhaps less attractive, side of Reacher's individualism. It emerges during the prison chapters, when he is initially reluctant to lift a finger to help Hubble. In Chapter 6, he actually says that he doesn't care what happens to Hubble. He then allows the gang members to threaten his cellmate for a long time without intervening. The rationale that Reacher gives when he does intervene is less than public-spirited.

> Time to intervene. Not for Hubble. I felt nothing for him. But I had to intervene for myself. Hubble's abject performance would taint me. We would be seen as a pair. Hubble's surrender would disqualify us both. In the status game.

It's all about 'me' – selfish individualism.

Reacher's individualism is closely related to his anti-authoritarianism. We get an insight into his feelings about authority in Chapter 8, during a prison conversation with Hubble.

> 'Who the hell's after you?'
> 'Nobody,' I said. 'It's just a bit of fun. I like anonymity. I feel like I'm beating the system. And right now, I'm truly pissed at the system.'

Elsewhere, he reveals an aversion to situations that involve law enforcement. When Finlay presses him for any information that Hubble may have let slip in prison, he refuses to pass on what he knows, even though it could be useful to the investigation.

> I didn't answer. I wasn't entirely sure whose side I was on yet.

Basically, Reacher has a trust issue with authority figures.

This anti-authoritarianism persists long after Reacher actually does start collaborating with the police. His only reason for working alongside them, initially at least, is to pursue his own agenda, namely his mission to take revenge on the murderers and finish Joe's business. This is made abundantly clear in Chapter 15.

> I couldn't rely on Roscoe or Finlay. I couldn't expect either of them to agree with my agenda.

But it's important to understand that, in Reacher's eyes, this suspicion of the police is not immoral, or even amoral. In fact, he considers his own unorthodox and illegal methods a much more reliable way of achieving justice. Finlay and Roscoe can't be relied on because they are shackled to standard policing methods. By contrast, he has no restrictions, and, as he explains, that makes him much better positioned to deal with evil.

> I had no laws to worry about, no inhibitions, no distractions. I wouldn't have to think about Miranda, probable cause, constitutional rights. I wouldn't have to think about reasonable doubt or rules of evidence. No appeal to any higher authority for these guys. Was that fair? You bet your ass. These were bad people. They'd stepped over the line a long time ago.

The distrust is mutual. The police characters and Reacher are clearly like cat and dog. In Chapter 11, Finlay says that he thinks Reacher doesn't really care about the latest murder, in spite of his expression of interest.

> 'So what's the story?' I said.
> He lifted his head up with an effort and looked at me.
> 'Why should you care?' he said. 'What was he to you?'

Brotherhood

Reacher's individualism goes a long way to explaining his charm as a character, but, as we've seen, it does have a less attractive side. In the prison chapters, he's dangerously close to looking like a jerk when he sits on his hands while Hubble is victimised. Taking on the bad guys purely out of self-interest isn't much better either. Reacher has to change, and we know instinctively that he will.

There is, of course, a massive adjustment coming for Jack Reacher's individualism: the news of his brother's murder. In a long reflection after the identification of Joe's body, Reacher reveals that he and his brother barely communicated. They hadn't seen one another for seven years, and even then, it was only for their mother's funeral. He didn't even know whether his brother was married, or whether he'd started to lose his hair, as we hear during the interview with Finlay in Chapter 10. In fact, Reacher realises, in Chapter 25, that Kelstein knew Joe much better than he did. It's individualism of a rather sad and lonely kind, and probably all too familiar to a lot of readers. And yet, Reacher still feels the tug of loyalty. We hear from Kelstein that Joe Reacher talked about his brother a great deal.

> 'Good luck, Mr. Reacher,' he said. 'I hope you finish your brother's business. Perhaps you will. He spoke of you often. He liked you, you know.'
> 'He spoke of me?' I said.
> 'Often,' the old guy said again. 'He was very fond of you. He was sorry your job kept you so far away.'
> For a moment I couldn't speak. I felt unbearably guilty. Years would pass, I wouldn't think about him. But he was thinking about me?
> 'He was older, but you looked after him,' he said. "That's what Joe told me. He said you were very fierce. Very tough. I guess if Joe wanted anybody to take care of the Kliners, he'd have nominated

you.'
I nodded.

It seems Joe didn't build his personality around individualism in quite the same way as Jack did. It's even hinted that Joe sent his brother that message about Blind Blake knowing he would come to Margrave. Did Joe suspect that he was about to be killed? It's not discussed. But, even so, it's a poignant gesture of intimacy to reach out to your estranged brother. The result of the gesture is that Reacher undergoes a shift in his values. Soon after the discovery of Joe's murder, he makes it very clear that he won't settle until he has taken revenge and completed his brother's investigation.

> I was going to stand up for him. I was going to finish his business. Whatever it was. Whatever it took.

From the reader's perspective, the main problem with Reacher's initial selfish individualism was that it got in the way of the kind of experience that readers like – a difficult challenge overcome with skill and resolve. When Reacher starts to adopt the values of brotherhood and loyalty, it's exactly what the reader wants to see. When Reacher makes his fraternal vow of revenge, we can immediately imagine how the stakes are going to rise.

Reacher's personal transformation makes the vow even more dramatically enticing. If Reacher had been close buddies with Joe from the start of the novel, we wouldn't have been nearly so pumped up by his revenge mission. Transformation – especially for the better – is fascinating to readers and makes us root for the character involved. Perhaps it's because we hope to be redeemed from our own weaknesses on some unconscious level. Or perhaps it's even simpler than that. Maybe it's just that having something good withheld for a while makes it all the sweeter when it's finally given to you.

Many novels that include a transformation of the main character's values leave it until much later. It's often their last-gasp effort, coming after many chapters of comprehensive failure. But in *Killing Floor*, the transformation is what makes the plot possible. In fact, it becomes one of the keys to Reacher's success. In Chapter 19, for example, it's his knowledge of his brother's way of thinking that allows him to find a scrap of paper missed by Kliner's henchmen.

> 'OK, Joe,' I said to myself. 'Let's see if you were a smart guy.'
> I was looking for the shoes. They were in the outside pocket of the bag. Two pairs. Four shoes, just like it said on the housekeeper's list. I pulled the inner soles out of each one in turn. Under the third one, I found a tiny Ziploc bag. With a sheet of computer paper folded up inside it.
> 'Smart as a whip, Joe,' I said to myself, and laughed.

Anti-authoritarian Authoritarianism

Unlike Reacher's individualism, his anti-authoritarianism doesn't give way to a competing set of values. However, it does undergo a change of meaning.

As the novel proceeds, Reacher's anti-authoritarian values actually spread out into the cast of characters – at least among his allies. Surprisingly, it doesn't take much to make Finlay receptive. In Chapter 12, he talks to Reacher about his arrival in Margrave and expresses extreme dislike of the town's mayor. In fact, the whole town wreaks of moneyed privilege in his view.

> 'Town mayor appoints the chief of police. He's coming over. Guy named Teale. Some kind of an old Georgia family. Some ancestor was a railroad baron who owned everything in sight around here.'
> 'Is that the guy you've got statues of?' I said.
> Finlay nodded.
> 'Caspar Teale,' he said. 'He was the first. They've had Teales here ever since. This mayor must be the great-grandson or something.'
> I was in a minefield. I needed to find a clear lane through.
> 'What's the story with this guy Teale?' I asked him.
> Finlay shrugged. Tried to find a way to explain it.
> 'He's just a southern asshole,' he said. 'Old Georgia family, probably a long line of southern assholes. They've been the mayors around here since the beginning. I dare say this one's no worse than the others.'

Finlay's description implies that there is a racist side to the Teales. Reacher picks up on it and amplifies the sentiment.

> The town was run by some old Georgia type who couldn't remember slavery had been abolished.

By Chapter 14, both Finlay and Roscoe are actively conspiring behind Teale's back. Official police business (the hunt for Morrison's killer) has become totally side-lined. Roscoe is equally willing to break the rules. In Chapter 16, she provides Reacher with an illegal gun. Molly too, in perhaps the most daring disobedience of all, leaks details of the Treasury investigation that Joe was involved in.

What makes this spread of anti-authoritarianism possible is a growing realisation among Reacher's allies that many aspects of the fictional world are, quite literally, counterfeit or morally bankrupt, including the police department of Margrave. The only decent expression of authority in such circumstances is an anti-authoritarian one – or so Reacher, Finlay and Roscoe conclude. Chapter 21 is one of the key moments. It's then that Roscoe and Reacher realise Detective Gray was murdered by his own colleagues. The effect on her worldview is devastating.

> 'I was at his funeral,' she said. 'We were all there. Chief Morrison made a speech on the lawn outside the church. So did Mayor Teale. They said he was a fine officer. They said he was Margrave's finest. But they killed him.'
> She said it with a lot of feeling. She'd liked Margrave. Her family had toiled there for generations. She was rooted. She'd liked her job. Enjoyed the sense of contribution. But the community she'd served was rotten. It was dirty and corrupted. It wasn't a community. It was a swamp, wallowing in dirty money and blood. I sat and watched her world crumble.

In the last chapter, I showed how the gradual unmasking of a rotten society is one means by which Lee Child motivates his main character to raise the stakes. It's a simple mechanism: the bigger the threat, the more likely a hero is to run towards it. And what threat could possibly be bigger than a whole class of authority figures who murder and counterfeit to enrich themselves? It puts Reacher's anti-authoritarianism in a completely new light: less revolutionary and more conservative; more about restoring due authority than resisting it. At the end of the novel, we are certainly left with the feeling that his actions have redeemed society. Roscoe sums up the feeling of renewal.

> 'This is my town and I'm going to be really involved in it. Maybe

I'll get on the town board. Maybe I'll even run for mayor. That would be a hell of a thing, wouldn't it? After all these years, a Roscoe for mayor, instead of a Teale?'

This anti-authoritarian authoritarianism of Reacher's is a perfect example of how a main character's values have a powerful influence over a novel. They even determine the level of the stakes. Consequently, an author has to ensure that those values will plausibly motivate the hero to go out on a limb in highly public ways. I would even say that the character's principled struggle must resonate on a universal level with a very wide readership. So, if you're thinking of creating a series of novels around a character whose main virtue is tidiness, perhaps you had better think again.

Other Antis

A couple of very specific social values intertwine with Reacher's anti-authoritarianism. Specifically, there is a strong streak of both anti-racism and anti-capitalism in his characterisation.

Reacher's antipathy to capitalism emerges in details. For example, on several occasions, his eye falls on information about government cutbacks, especially in the customs service. In Chapter 2, it's casually slipped into a scene about other things when Reacher happens to read a news story on the subject. The same strategy is used in Chapter 8. In Chapter 5, there is a brief exchange about prison cutbacks that further reveals Reacher's sensitivity to the subject.

It's not just about cutbacks. There are many other moments when Reacher's anti-capitalism comes through. When he's under arrest and travelling in a patrol car back to Margrave police headquarters, he looks out of the window and briefly wonders who works the land and how just that arrangement is.

Did people own their land here. Or did giant corporations?

Later, when Hubble walks into the police headquarters for the first time, he describes him as 'a man who wallowed in the yuppie dream like a pig in shit.' This anti-capitalist sentiment resonates particularly strongly with the whydunnit question at the heart of the plot. As we saw in a previous chapter, the novel casts wealth and privilege in a very dark light. So dark that they are the defining characteristics of killers and counterfeiters.

A mass of throwaway lines provides us with the fine detail of Reacher's values. In addition to the anti-capitalist sentiments already mentioned, he makes a number of statements in the early chapters of *Killing Floor* that indicate a certain sensitivity to race issues. In Chapter 2, he describes Finlay (with cutting irony) as 'Like a Boston banker except black.' In Chapter 6, he speculates, with the same cynical tone, that an old black man he encounters in prison must be doing sixty years for stealing a chicken.

As I suggested at the start of this chapter, in order to maintain interest in a series hero who is the embodiment of a big, highly general value – freedom in Reacher's case – it helps if each novel's plot foregrounds and examines one or two facets of that value. In *Killing Floor*, Reacher's anti-capitalist and anti-racist views are two of the aspects of freedom under consideration. The fact that both concepts have a rather problematic relationship with the historical realities of freedom and enslavement only helps to increase the drama level in the novel. What could be more problematic than the relationship between freedom, on the one hand, and capitalism or race relations on the other hand? The turbulence between these three ideas kicks up a mass of moral questions, and they swirl around at the edge of the reader's consciousness in the course of the novel. Here are just a few.

- Is the wealth that makes us a free society undermining the fabric of our society?
- If our current freedom is built on the historic enslavement of black people, has that left traces?
- Are we truly free if we are chained to jobs and possessions?
- Does a free country always use its freedom wisely?

Themes

What is the distinction between values and themes? For current purposes, values are the attitudes espoused by a character in the novel. A theme, by contrast, is an attitude expressed through the novel, but not associated with a character's thoughts and actions. If you like, characters have no 'knowledge' of theme.

That doesn't mean that themes are completely unrelated to

values. Often, the two are very closely bound up. It's as though the fictional world around the characters echoes back the values that motivate them. This happens through a myriad of details, both small and large, which resonate with one another and with the main character's values to suggest a meaning beyond themselves. In a novel with first-person narration, like *Killing Floor*, this occurs more naturally than in a third-person-narrated novel because the narrator's viewpoint openly determines our perception of the fictional world.

Let's take a look at just a few of the theme-relevant details that resonate with Reacher's values.

Freedom is the most general value associated with Reacher, and, almost inevitably, it's picked up as a theme. The idea of freedom (and its associated problems) is hinted at by various details of the text. For example, in Chapter 9, a section ends with the image of a road that is 'going nowhere'. The implication is that you can have all the freedom in the world, but if you have no sense of direction, it'll do you no good. The image is the very essence of Reacher's free-spirited lifestyle, but it also lifts the freedom debate beyond the character's narrow concerns, addressing a national or even universal human problem: rudderlessness at the personal and the political level.

Each of the values expressed by Reacher receives some kind of thematic commentary. In the case of Reacher's new-found sense of brotherly connection to Joe, the commentary comes in the form of an inverted reflection. When Lee Child wrote the prison chapters, he didn't have to specify that the most violent gang in the place was the Aryan Brotherhood, but the thematic possibilities of the name were clearly just too tempting. As a phrase, it suggests that the group is a brotherhood based on false principles. Their bond of hatred is the polar opposite of the bond that Reacher rediscovers: a strong connection of duty and understanding.

Reacher's other values receive the same kind of thematic commentary. The Margrave environment is full of details that cause us to reflect on individualism, specifically as it relates to capitalism. In Chapter 10, the street on which Hubble lives is described. Its houses get further and further apart as you head out of the centre. They are massive, plush piles. surrounded by acres of isolating space. It's difficult not to see that as a comment on the way wealth undermines community.

We heard earlier that Reacher is sensitised to the issue of government cuts, and notices repeatedly that this is affecting the customs service. Later, as the criminal investigation works itself out, it becomes clear that the lack of an effective customs service had a key role in enabling the movement of counterfeit money. This is just one example of how the crime story in *Killing Floor* produces image after image that throws light on Reacher's values. In this case, it is his anti-capitalism that gets lifted onto the thematic stage. The conspirators and the customs officials become emblematic of capitalism and anti-capitalism.

Details commenting on Reacher's anti-racist values are even more prevalent. In fact, they are the pillar of a whole subplot, which will be discussed in the next chapter.

As with many aspects of thriller writing, these brief details that cast a light on important themes are most effective when they occur at plot points. The definitive example in *Killing Floor* is the mass of detail that builds up during the raid on the Kliner warehouse, creating a veritable tsunami of anti-capitalist thematics. To give just a few examples, Lee Child waits thirty-three chapters to reveal the interior of the building where Joe Reacher was murdered, building and building our anticipation before showing us a mountain of money. Not only that, but the money is being shovelled by enslaved workers. Then finally, of course, the defeat of the criminals coincides with a massive conflagration that destroys the money mountain and scatters notes all over the surrounding area – to the delight of the locals. It's a literary socialist revolution!

The plot points of a good thriller should all be resonating with the novel's theme, but the climactic scene should be almost allegorical in the way its details broadcast the novel's moral 'message'. It's the closest we should get to hearing the author speak his mind. But the only way an author can get away with that is if the story has been so compelling up to that point that the reader can't help but go along with their allegory. The climactic scene is your prize for working hard at creating a compelling main character and situations that validate their values, while also providing a gentle commentary on those values with resonant details.

Takeaway

- A main character's values should be chosen for maximum dramatic potential. Ideally the character should undergo some moral change.

- Because he is writing a series, Lee Child makes his main character an embodiment of a single, very general value. He then uses each book in the series to examine facets of that value.

- Reacher's values are challenged by circumstances in the novel. Under pressure, he experiences some moral change. Other aspects of his value system remain intact, but appear in a new light as circumstances change around them.

- Lee Child has chosen to foreground moral positions that have a problematic relationship with the general value embodied by the main character.

- The text is scattered with details that comment on the main character's moral values. They are concentrated at plot points, especially the climactic scene.

8. STORYTELLING

'Blind Blake was a guitar player,' I said. 'Died sixty years ago, maybe
murdered. My brother bought a record, sleeve note said it happened in
Margrave. He wrote me about it. Said he was through here a couple of
times in the spring, some kind of business. I thought I'd come down and
check the story out.'
- Lee Child, *Killing Floor*

There's a myth that some people are simply good tellers of tales
and some are not. People will often say about themselves 'Oh, I
can't even tell a joke'. Other people seem to hold the room when
they relate an anecdote. But I'm here to tell you that anyone can
learn better storytelling. It's all about releasing information in the
right way and at the right time.

Set-up and Pay-off

One of the most striking things about the storytelling in *Killing
Floor*, is that the author keeps giving us little hints at things that will
come later in the plot. This is a common writing technique, often
described using the terms 'set-up' and 'pay-off'. The set-up is any
moment when the author provides a pre-echo of events that will
happen later in the story. The pay-off is the moment when your
expectations are fulfilled.

In *Killing Floor*, there are a huge number of set-ups and pay-
offs. Often, they relate to the investigative activities being carried
out by Reacher and co. The set-up hints at some part of the truth

about the criminal conspiracy and the pay-off confirms it. But this is not as unsubtle as it seems. Lee Child is an expert at creating set-ups that give you a nagging anxiety – not quite a full-blown suspicion but a vague, almost-unconscious awareness of danger or hidden information. In Chapter 7, for example, we hear from Hubble about the last head detective of Margrave – how he apparently killed himself.

> 'There's only eight people in the whole police department. Chief Morrison, he's been there years, then the desk man, four uniformed men, a woman, and the detective, Gray. Only now it's Finlay. The new man. Black guy, the first we've ever had. Gray killed himself, you know. Hung himself from a rafter in his garage. February, I think.'

It's a strange digression, and it leaves us wondering whether there was more to Gray's death than meets the eye. In Chapter 22, this suspicion is paid off when Gray's notes and a visit to the pathologist more or less confirm that he was murdered. This fifteen-chapter interval between set-up and pay-off is not unusual, although there are many examples of shorter spans. The longer the span, the greater the thrill when the pay-off actually occurs. It's an effect very similar to those strung out questions that we heard about in a previous chapter.

Other examples include the mention of Reacher's brother during the first interview with Finlay (paid off seven chapters later when the brother appears on the pathologist's slab), also the moment when Roscoe is asked to go and stand in for Picard at the safe house (paid off six chapters later when Picard shows his true colours) and Hubble's mention of his passion for the Beatles (paid off twenty-six chapters later when Reacher finds him living under the name Paul Lennon).

The purpose of this technique is partly to increase the reader's anticipation. This keeps them turning the pages. But it also gives the reader a feeling that there is an underlying structure to the novel's mystery. That helps them to relax and allow themselves to be entertained. Finally, depending how obvious the set-up is, it may also flatter the reader's sense of their own intelligence and predictive powers.

In addition to the set-up / pay-off structures that relate to the investigation, there are some that have no connection to the novel's mystery whatsoever. For example, when Hubble walks into the police headquarters, Reacher speculates that he's wearing brown boat shoes or some such yuppie attire. His suspicions are confirmed almost immediately, and he remarks on it again two chapters later, when they're languishing in a prison cell together. This set-up and pay-off is quite simply funny, and makes us even more enamoured of the novel's main character and his anti-establishment values.

These set-up and pay-off structures might seem tiny and insignificant, but we begin to appreciate their importance on the rare occasions when Lee Child fails to provide either a set-up or a pay-off. Consider Reacher's outburst of joy as he triumphs over the conspirators in Chapter 33.

> Thirty-six years of bad luck and trouble were wiped away in one single bright glance.

It rings hollow because, up to that point, the novel has given us no real indication that Reacher's life has been particularly troubled. Unsettled, yes, but quite happy with his life – until the military dispensed with him. Even then, he seems to have made the best of his enforced retirement, choosing to live on his own terms rather than answering to an employer. Maybe there are other events that we don't know about, but the end of a novel is a place for pay-offs, not set-ups. It's a rare false step in the storytelling.

Narrator Takes the Lead

In a way, set-ups and pay-offs are a way of letting the reader temporarily feel that they're ahead of the novel's main character in their understanding of events. If we're alert to details, we can even start to make successful predictions about the plot direction in *Killing Floor*. But allowing that to happen all the time would never do. A thriller must, of course, outsmart the reader in the end. But it must do so only just. The readers must be encouraged to think that the solution to the mystery is within their grasp, but then find themselves left for standing by the main character at key moments.

This is exactly what Lee Child achieves. There are a number of moments when Reacher acts without explaining himself. It's generally at moments when the challenges facing him seem almost insurmountable. For example, in Chapter 26, Reacher raids the closet at Hubble's home without explaining what it is he plans to do. We know he needs equipment, but the purpose remains a mystery. Subsequently we see the equipment in action, and Reacher brings us up to speed by providing a running commentary on how to carry out an ambush. Being temporarily ahead of Reacher may flatter our egos, but being behind him gives us a thrill too – a sense that we are in the presence of an exceptional individual.

Such episodes happen more frequently as the climax of the novel approaches. In Chapter 27, Reacher is again staying over at Hubble's place. He reads deeply into the subject of cash movements – something that Hubble has a large collection of literature about. In the morning, after a long night of reading, he's very excited. He clearly has an answer to a question that has been bugging him: where do the counterfeiters get their paper. However, he doesn't let us into the secret. He even teases Finlay before revealing it.

> 'Get dressed. We're going somewhere.'
> 'Going where?' he said.
> 'Atlanta,' I said. 'Something to show you.'
> 'What something?' he said. 'Just tell me, can't you?'
> 'Get dressed, Finlay,' I said again. 'Got to go.'

Similarly, Reacher gets ahead of us in Chapter 33 when he sits down to eat and plan what to do about the kidnapping of Roscoe and Charlie. Later, we see him pushing a fork into the tyre of the car, but we have no idea what he is planning to do when the tyre goes flat. Eventually, Reacher's plan to kill Picard and the other henchmen becomes apparent.

Pace

It's not immediately obvious how a sense of pace is created in a written text. After all, the reader reads at whatever speed they like – it's different for each individual. However, there are techniques by which an author can create an illusion that time is passing in a rapid blur. Almost magically, the reader will find themselves speeding up in their actual turning of the pages. This is extremely useful as a way of getting the reader to engage deeply with moments of tension. Quite literally, you want their hearts to start beating faster when things are tense for the hero.

In the first chapter of *Killing Floor*, we're launched straight into a moment of relative tension as we read how Reacher is arrested and taken to the police precinct. The scene moves at a steady pace, but without the frenetic quality of some later passages. This is a clever trick if you can pull it off, as the reader will be encouraged to turn the pages quickly, but won't get exhausted too soon. That makes it perfect for the start of a novel. The characteristics of the text at this stage are as follows.

- Tiny details are reported, such as the stance and positioning of each arresting officer and the capabilities of each weapon. Together they add up to a relatively small amount of activity spread over a longish period of reading time. It gives the impression of a highly acute mind taking in complex events and immediately comprehending them. It's rather like a high-speed camera capturing rapid motion so that it can produce a smooth slow-motion replay (a technique commonly used in action cinema).

  > The guy with the revolver stayed at the door. He went into a crouch and pointed the weapon two-handed. At my head. The guy with the shotgun approached close. These were fit lean boys. Neat and tidy. Textbook moves. The revolver at the door could cover the room with a degree of accuracy. The shotgun up close could splatter me all over the window.

- Reacher's thoughts dwell on some of the details, even though they're supposedly happening in quick time. It's like that moment in *Matrix* when the hero steps outside of events and closely observes a bullet racing past him. Here's an example.

  > I just sat and watched them. I knew who was in the diner. A cook in back. Two waitresses. Two old men. And me. This operation was for me. I had been in town less than a half hour. The other five had probably been here all their lives. Any problem with any of them and an embarrassed sergeant would have shuffled in. He would be apologetic. He would mumble to them. He would ask them to come down to the station house. So the heavy weapons and the rush weren't

for any of them.

- The details just keep coming. That gives a sense of movement to the text. However, many of the details reported are not exactly dynamic – stuff like the contents of Reacher's plate – so the energy of the text remains steady and flowing.

> I WAS ARRESTED IN ENO'S DINER. AT TWELVE O'CLOCK. I was eating eggs and drinking coffee. A late breakfast, not lunch. I was wet and tired after a long walk in heavy rain. All the way from the highway to the edge of town.
> The diner was small, but bright and clean. Brand-new, built to resemble a converted railroad car. Narrow, with a long lunch counter on one side and a kitchen bumped out back. Booths lining the opposite wall. A doorway where the center booth would be.

- The language used is relatively unemotional and unenergised. This also helps to keep the energy of the text to a steady flow rather than a raging torrent.

> So far, they were doing it right. No doubt about that. They had the advantage. No doubt about that, either. The tight booth trapped me. I was too hemmed in to do much. I spread my hands on the table.

- The sentences are mostly very short. In fact, heavy use of full stops often breaks the text into fragments even shorter than a sentence. This makes us feel we're within the perceptions of a person who is really experiencing the events, even though that person is using the past tense.

> They were moving fast and crunched to a stop. Light bars flashing and popping. Red and blue light in the raindrops on my window. Doors burst open, policemen jumped out. Two from each car, weapons ready. Two revolvers, two shotguns.

Because Reacher is the narrator of the text, the slow and steady pace is implicitly the pace of his thoughts. It's a clever choice by

Lee Child to keep the text on a leash, because it gives us the perfect introduction to Reacher's cool and capable personality.

Contrast that passage with the description of the prison riot in Chapter 7 – a much more frenetic affair. The characteristics of the text at that point are as follows.

- The same short sentence fragments are used. Perhaps even shorter. It puts us directly behind Reacher's eyes once again. These staccato utterances deliver the same continuous, energised flow of details as the Eno's diner passage.

  > Boots clattered. Shouting and screaming. Sirens. We raced to the cell. Fell inside. I was dizzy and panting. I had taken a battering. The sirens were deafening. Couldn't talk.

- The vocabulary is much more energised than in the description of the arrest at the diner. Look at the verbs: 'hustled', 'blasting', 'tumbling', 'clattered', 'shouting', 'screaming', 'raced', 'fell', 'panting'.

- There is a lot of repetition – specifically of a very simple sentence structure using the word 'I'. This gives the impression that Reacher's rational faculties have been temporarily switched off.

  > I saw Hubble bouncing around in the crowd. I saw guards. I saw hundreds of men. I saw Spivey.

- The details are small, as in the Eno's diner passage. But unlike the diner passage, they are disconnected, and quite a lot of action is covered by a small number of sentences, creating a hastier effect.

After these breathless passages of frenetic action, Lee Child is careful to bring the pace down and give the reader a rest. You can't make people sprint-read for too long without exhausting them.

The characteristics of a really unpacy passage in *Killing Floor* are typified by Reacher's reflection on the death of his brother, at the start of Chapter 10.

- It shows the same fragmentation of grammar, but with longer and more complex sentences. Complex Jack Reacher sentences are still not very complex by other people's standards, but there is at least one sentence that contains two conjunctions: 'We were only two years apart, but he was born in the fifties and I was born in the sixties.'

- We see more abstract and undynamic vocabulary. For example: 'The truth was I never knew for sure if I loved him or not.' Love, truth, knowledge, certainty – it's all very different from the cold, hard facts that Reacher usually utters.

- The passage is all about reflection rather than action. For example: 'I loved him like a brother. But that phrase has a very precise [sic] meaning. A lot of those stock sayings do. Like when people say they slept like a baby. Do they mean they slept well? Or do they mean they woke up every ten minutes, screaming?' Strange ruminations of that kind are not unknown elsewhere in the novel, but this is probably the strangest and most ruminative.

As the climax of the novel approaches, one would expect the prose to become more and more frenzied, but something strange happens instead. Let's consider how the warehouse-raid scene in Chapter 33 is narrated. The energy and pace certainly do seem to build through the scene. We see all the same tricks: simple sentences beginning 'I', fragmentary utterances, repetition of phrases like 'was screaming', and so on. But at the absolute climax of the action, it's as though we are in the eye of the storm. We go into maximum slow motion with micro-detail as Reacher tries to bring his gun to bear faster than the enemy. It draws out the suspense almost beyond endurance. The energy from the earlier part of the passage, combined with this sudden slowness makes us race through the text, desperate to know the outcome. It's worth quoting the whole passage in full.

> After that, my brain just shut down. Handed me all that information and sat back to mock my attempt to haul my arm up faster than Kliner could haul the Ithaca's barrel up. It was a race in agonizing slow motion. I was leaning half off the balcony

slowly bringing my arm up as if I was lifting an enormous weight. A hundred feet away Kliner was slowly raising the shotgun barrel as if it was mired in molasses. They came up together, slowly, inch by inch, degree by degree. Up and up. It took forever. It took the whole of my lifetime. Flames were bursting and exploding at the bottom of the mountain. They were spreading upward and outward through the money. Kliner's yellow teeth were parting in a wolfish smile. Charlie was screaming. Roscoe was slowly floating down toward the concrete floor like gossamer. My arm and Kliner's shotgun were traveling slowly upward together, inch by ghastly inch.

My arm got there first. I fired and hit Kliner in the right upper chest and the huge .44 slug hurled him off his feet. The Ithaca barrel whipped sideways as he pulled the trigger. The shotgun boomed and fired point-blank into the enormous mountain of money. The air was instantly thick with tiny scraps of paper. Shreds and fragments of dollar bills were blasted all over the place. They swirled like a thick blizzard and burst into flames as they settled into the fire.

Then time restarted...

Suddenly, we are through the moment of maximum danger and maximum story significance, and it's back into simple energetic sentences. The chapter races to its end.

Something few writers about writing notice is that there are different types of pace. Until now, we have been describing pacy action that is designed to get the pulse racing and the pages turning. But there is also pacy summary. This is designed to get the reader through a necessary but somewhat uninteresting phase of the novel. For example, in Chapter 8, we're given a montage of summarised dialogue. It explains how Reacher was exonerated. The main difference between this kind of paciness and thrilling paciness is the relative lack of detail. The events are not described in a vivid fashion. Only their general outlines are evoked.

We were having a good time. We drank a lot of beer, sat tight together in the booth. Then we danced for a while. Couldn't resist it. The band played on and on. The room got hot and crowded. The music got louder and faster. The waitresses sprinted back and forth with long-neck bottles.

This technique is rarely used in *Killing Floor*. After all, the ideal situation is for your story to contain no dead zones that need to be skipped through.

That said, I should note that pace isn't everything. Marching readers through the novel at top speed is not the only technique an author can use to get us to the end of the story. On any journey, it's good to have a map that shows you where you are and where you're going. Lee Child does a good job of that. He does so by providing both context reminders and directions. Again and again, the characters pause to take stock of what is happening and what's coming next – information that helps the reader get their bearings. This always happens organically, in the course of events. Sometimes it occurs when Reacher is travelling and reflecting on the investigation. At other times, it's a group thing. For example, in Chapter 13, Reacher, Finlay and Roscoe have a mini-summit to discuss what activities they need to undertake. It orients us for the next few chapters. In Chapter 17, there's another meeting that provides a full update on what activities the characters are involved in and – crucially – what obstacles stand in their way. Roscoe also clearly states what she will be moving onto next. In Chapter 19, we get yet another update. The characters discuss the fact that certain recent activities have yet to produce fruit. These map-reading sessions clarify the reader's understanding of actions and motivations during the most complicated stages of the investigation.

Chapters

Chapters are usually the main building block of a novel. In the work of some authors, they are highly structured affairs – almost like well-crafted stories in their own right. This is not the case with *Killing Floor*, which is divided up into chapters in an almost arbitrary way. Each begins where the last ended, and their contents don't seem to have any real structure. They sometimes end on a cliffhanger, but that's the closest Lee Child gets to designing his chapters.

This is a valid way of using chapters. After all, one of the main reasons for having them is simply to give the reader somewhere to stop conveniently. They also help you to judge your progress through the novel. Both of those things are achieved by the *Killing Floor* chapter divisions.

Some of the cliffhangers are, in any case, highly effective.

There are different types. Firstly, the noisy variety. With these, a chapter rises to a dramatic, suspenseful moment, and in the following chapter there is a quieter response to the drama. For example, at the end of Chapter 2, we discover that Chief Morrison himself is giving damning testimony against Reacher. In Chapter 3, Reacher has to set about establishing an alibi. There is also an inverted type of cliffhanger. With these, chapters end with a reference to some nagging problem, and in the following chapter the problem materialises in full force. They go from quiet to noisy and dramatic, rather than the other way round. For example, Chapter 17 ends with Reacher being followed as he leaves the police headquarters. Chapter 18 picks up with Reacher setting a violent ambush for the men shadowing him.

Even when there is no particular cliffhanger, any event that occurs at the end of a chapter acquires an exaggerated significance. Lee Child exploits this on several occasions. For example, at the end of Chapter 10, it's reported that Hubble had still not called Reacher back. His disappearance is an issue that will go on to acquire extreme importance in the novel, but at this early stage, the author just subtly suggests what's to come. The end of the chapter has an effect like the theme from the twilight zone.

Chapters that lack an internal structure are in danger of becoming dull. They begin at point A and end at point B, and there's no sense of arriving at a destination after a journey. I think that's probably why Lee Child has a tendency to interrupt scenes with a completely unrelated observation – something that hints at a plot development yet to come. It disrupts the predictable flow of the story and creates a landmark, like a distant view of the town you're travelling towards. In many places, Reacher spots the black pickup of the Kliner boy while he's in the middle of something else. He also bumps into both Teale and Kliner at the police headquarters on separate occasions. He exchanges unpleasantries with them before returning to the activity he was engaged in.

Earlier, we looked at the role of sentences in creating pace. We concluded that they tend to become more staccato at moments of dramatic action. Scenes work a bit differently. At moments that are in danger of becoming dull, it's good practice to keep the scenes short. Chapter 17, for example, contains quite a large number of chapters, because it's largely an account of workmanlike investigative activities. By contrast, Chapter 33, the climax of the novel, really contains just one extended scene. You could think of it as a macro-version of the 'eye-of-the-storm' effect discussed above.

As regards length, the chapters of *Killing Floor* may have a slight tendency to become longer after early plot points (e.g. Chapter 10 after the discovery of Joe's murder, and Chapter 16 after the invasion of Roscoe's home) and shorter at moments of high drama (e.g. Chapter 1 when Reacher is arrested, and Chapter 28 when Picard is revealed as a traitor) but there's no pronounced pattern.

Subplots

There are two subplots in *Killing Floor*. I'll refer to them as the romance plot and the race plot. They serve completely different purposes within the novel, but both contribute significantly to its success.

Let's consider the romance plot first.

Sex and romance are fiendishly difficult subjects to write about, but the relationship between Reacher and Roscoe is one of the many things about *Killing Floor* that seems to hook readers – especially female readers. Naturally, the only evidence I have for that assertion is anecdotal, given that I'm a man, so it's possible you'll radically disagree. But hear me out! For what it's worth, I believe one of the main reasons for the success of this subplot is the sympathetic depiction of Roscoe. She's active, intelligent and detailed as a character. In addition, it seems to me that Roscoe and Reacher relate to one another in a way that's calculated to appeal to female readers. If it's true, that's not an insignificant factor, given that the majority of thriller readers are women. So, for example, in Chapter 4, both Reacher and Roscoe admire one another's eyes within the space of a few hundred words.

> 'You're welcome,' she said, and she smiled, with her eyes too. I smiled back. Her eyes were like a welcome blast of sunshine on a rotten afternoon.
> …
> 'You don't match the deviance profile.'
> 'I don't?' I said.
> 'I could tell right away.' She smiled. 'You got nice eyes.'
> She winked and walked away.

The repetition of that one specific behaviour makes me sure it's a deliberate calibration – apparently for a female audience. On a similar note, Reacher is not afraid to show vulnerability under the right circumstances, and Roscoe seems to see it as a positive thing. When Reacher's coming to terms with the death of his brother in Chapter 10, for example, she takes his hand and comforts him.

Puzzlingly, there's also a good deal of red-blooded detail in Lee Child's depiction of Roscoe and the relationship – features that would seem to undermine the softer, more feminised details described above. For example, while Roscoe is taking Reacher's fingerprints in Chapter 2, he notices her breasts resting on the table. In Chapter 19, in a hotel-room scene, it's quite another part of her body that he admires at length, much to Roscoe's pleasure.

But, here's an important point. As an author, you can give your viewpoint character just about any perception of the world you want, no matter how challenging to the reader, so long as you have first worked hard to establish that your character is a likeable person. By the time Reacher comes to have his fingerprints taken in Chapter 2, we've been exposed for some time to his calm, distinctively military, occasionally humorous and surprisingly socially engaged viewpoint. A little unreconstructed maleness is not going to detract from that in a hurry. In any case, this mix of red-blooded and less red-blooded just goes to show that we shouldn't make too many assumptions about what is and isn't acceptable behaviour for a male character in the eyes of readers, especially women. Why can't audiences be conflicted on the issue? Perhaps aspects of both red-blooded and less red-blooded are welcome. There's one particular scene that lends weight to this suggestion. After the invasion of Roscoe's home, we see Reacher playing the role of a strong male defender figure.

> Roscoe put her hand to her mouth and gave a silent gasp. Her eyes were wide. They slid from the door to me.
> I grabbed her elbow and pulled her away.

On the face of it, it seems like another example of old-school, alpha-male behaviour. But on consideration, his actions have some softer features. He doesn't run around hitting the walls and vowing revenge. What he does do is show psychological sensitivity.

> Roscoe was following the trail of footprints. Showing a classic reaction. Denial. Four men had come to butcher her in the night. She knew that, but she was ignoring it. Closing it out of her mind. Dealing with it by not dealing with it. Not a bad approach, but she'd fall off the high wire before long. Until then, she was making herself busy tracing the faint footprints on her floors.

With great insight, he realises that what Roscoe needs most is to restore her sense of security. He deliberately pumps himself up with powerful words to show that she has an invincible force on her side.

> I knew I had to sound confident. Fear wouldn't get her anywhere. Fear would just sap her energy. She had to face it down. And she had to face down the dark and the quiet again tonight, and every other night of her life.
> 'I wish we had been here,' I said. 'We could have gotten a few answers.'

It's psychological sensitivity integrated with traditionally male protectiveness. I suspect that's exactly what Lee Child's fanbase likes.

Before we move on, I'd like to mention one factor that possibly mars the romance plot. It's the issue of Roscoe's professional credibility. Reacher begins well by treating Roscoe more or less as a professional equal. Investigative tasks are shared between them, and Reacher acknowledges Roscoe's excellence. Her theory explaining the movement of Kliner's trucks is seen as an important breakthrough by Finlay – a view that Reacher clearly shares.

> FINLAY NODDED. HE WAS CONVINCED. THEN HE SMILED. HE stood up from the bench in the barbershop window and took Roscoe's hand. Shook it very formally.
> 'Good work,' he said to her. 'A perfect analysis. I always said you were smart, Roscoe. Right, Reacher? Didn't I tell you she's the best we got?'
> I nodded and smiled and Roscoe blushed.

But what makes this dynamic even more attractive is the way their investigative talk sometimes merges with pillow talk. Roscoe leaves a note for Reacher after their first night together, for example. It's half affectionate, half business-like.

> There was a note propped against the pot. The note said: Early lunch at Eno's? Eleven o'clock? Leave Hubble to Finlay, OK? The note was signed with lots of kisses and a little drawing of a pair of handcuffs.

Also, in Chapter 19, we get an image of them going to bed but laying down their weapons as they do so.

> In the room we just crashed out. Roscoe laid her shiny .38 on the carpet on her side of the bed. I reloaded my giant .44 and laid it on my side. Cocked and locked.

His 'n' hers firearms. Cute!

So far so good. They make a lovely crime-fighting couple. But then something happens that saps the positivity from the relationship altogether: Picard dupes the good guys into sending Roscoe to an imaginary safe house. It takes her out of the picture completely from little more than half way through the novel, and it does so to no particular purpose. Having been a lover-collaborator, she becomes a mere damsel in distress, remaining so for eleven chapters. What a waste!

But leaving aside that misstep, let's consider the overall purpose of the romance subplot. How does it earn its place in the novel?

From almost the beginning of the relationship, it seems that Lee Child is subtly setting Roscoe up as a challenge to Reacher's individualism. When Reacher is picked up by Roscoe outside the prison, Hubble is picked up by his wife at the same time. The parallel immediately made me think: Where is this going? Elsewhere, we see them doing slightly mundane, couply things together. The meal they share in Chapter 18 is reported in a very unembellished fashion and completely without dialogue. It's almost like we're reading about a husband and wife. Even the scene in which they lay their weapons down beside the bed has a weird kind of domesticity. It poses a very interesting question: is a slightly twisted version of a normal relationship possible in Reacher's world?

Fascinating as the question is, the reader knows the answer long before they get it: of course not. Even a twisted version of a normal relationship is impossible in Reacher's world. The violent forces that he deals with are just too extreme. Roscoe gets abducted in spite of Reacher's best efforts – a fact that becomes an issue in their relationship, we are told in Chapter 34. And that's not the only area of friction between their two worlds. Apparently, Roscoe also felt that her lover went too far with the violence he dished out to Kliner's men. The message is very clear: Reacher lives in a world where normal people would curl up and die – that's what makes him a hero, but that's also what makes him lonely. So, we can see that the role of the romance plot is to highlight the importance of freedom, and especially individualism, in the character of Jack Reacher.

As we have seen, the race plot is the main expression of an important theme in *Killing Floor*. Allow me to recap. Reacher's values revolve around freedom, and when you break that down, you find that he has a strong anti-authoritarian streak. Cooperating with the police is anathema to him, and he describes himself as being 'truly pissed at the system'. His anti-authoritarianism is closely associated with a hatred of racism. Perhaps the clearest expression of that is when he jokes, cynically, that an old black man in prison is probably doing sixty years for stealing a chicken.

So, why are these particular values or views ascribed to Reacher? As I've said before, nothing is wasted in a good thriller. If it's there, it's there for a reason. In my view, Reacher's anti-racist views are there to cast an important critical light on the idea of freedom. The critique goes like this: We claim that our societies stand for liberty, but in the past, we allowed discrimination to curtail the freedom of black people. What does that say about our idea of freedom? This conflict becomes a major theme of the novel, since it is echoed by many aspects of the fictional world. Let's consider that in detail.

The figure of Blind Blake is at the heart of the race plot. Reacher's decision to visit Margrave is not random. It's not even down to the fact that he admires Blind Blake's guitar playing – although that is true. It's because he wanted to follow up on a story that Blind Blake was killed in Margrave, as we're told in Chapter 2.

> 'Blind Blake was a guitar player,' I said. 'Died sixty years ago, maybe murdered. My brother bought a record, sleeve note said it happened in Margrave. He wrote me about it. Said he was through

here a couple of times in the spring, some kind of business. I thought I'd come down and check the story out.'

When the barber subsequently takes up the subject of the murder, it becomes clear that it has a special significance in the novel. In any other literary genre, it could be mistaken for just another interesting background detail, but in a crime novel revolving around murder, it can only mean one thing: that the sixty-year-old killing of Blind Blake and the killings under investigation are linked in some way. I would argue that the link is a moral one, and that the main purpose of the race plot is to act as a moral commentary on the main plot.

The moral links between the race plot and the main plot are not difficult to discern. As the general corruption of society is unmasked by Reacher and his allies, an ugly streak of racism is also revealed. The characters who are marked out as obvious villains on account of their wealth and arrogance are also rooted in a historic culture of racial discrimination. We hear, for example, that there are no fewer than two statues to the ancestor of Mayor Teale who killed Blind Blake. Reacher, on several occasions, is leaning up against one of them while reflecting on the criminal conspiracy.

> We crossed the grass and leaned up on the statue of old Caspar Teale, side by side.
> 'They cut his balls off, right?' I said.

The eerie cleanness of the town – achieved through money laundering – is also symbolically linked to the statue.

> The bronze statue of old Caspar Teale looked like somebody licked it clean every morning.

But as we approach the end of the novel, hints and vague innuendos give way to a clear message. The true nature of the Teale family is laid bare for Reacher and the readers to see. It's an ugly moral legacy, and it encompasses both racism and lawless capitalism. The information is revealed in two important episodes.

Firstly, Roscoe reveals in Chapter 15 that her ancestors were dispossessed of land by the Teale family long ago.

> Some old ancestor had nearly made it big, but he lost his best land

when Mayor Teale's great-grandfather built the railroad. Then some mortgages were called in and the grudge rolled on down the years so that now she loved Margrave but hated to see Teale walking around like he owned it, which he did, and which Teales always had.

The anecdote confirms our impression that the Teales are predatory to the bone. But, the second, and more important unmasking of the Teale family is provided by the barber's sister in Chapter 32. At that point, just before the story climax, Reacher, Finlay and Hubble regroup in a location that's saturated with significance for the race plot: the barber's shop. It's very noticeable that, towards the end of *Killing Floor*, almost everything is saturated with thematic significance, but this setting is in a league of its own. It's so symbolically resonant that it's almost allegorical. It's a repository of memory about the black experience, it's where Gray chose to hide his research into the Margrave elites, it's the only business to refuse Kliner's dirty money and it's literally and morally the last light left burning in the town. In this special setting, the whole story of Blind Blake's murder is revealed. We learn that the barber's sister actually saw the musician being killed, and that she knows who did it. It was the father of Grover Teale (the current mayor). Interestingly, the account of the killing makes Grover Teale seem remarkably like the Kliner boy, mouthing off in the street. In every generation, it's suggested, the same social elite enforces its will.

> 'Who was the boy?' I asked her again.
> She turned to me and stared into my eyes. Told me the sixty-two-year-old secret.
> 'Grover Teale,' she said. 'Grew up to be mayor, just like his old daddy. Thinks he's king of the damn world, but he's just a screaming brat who got my poor Blake killed for no reason at all except he was blind and he was black.'

The episode completes this particular thread of moral commentary. Lee Child has made his case that racial discrimination, like greed, has the power to compromise liberty, even in societies that consider themselves free. But if you're in any doubt about the importance of the race plot as a moral commentary on the main character's values, consider this: the title chosen by Lee Child –

'Killing Floor' – is in fact the name of blues song by Howlin' Wolf.

The blues – a quintessentially black musical genre – pervades the novel. While Reacher is in the police cells, he uses his head stereo to play blues tracks to himself.

> To calm down, I ran music through my head. The chorus in 'Smokestack Lightning.' The Howling Wolf version puts a wonderful strangled cry on the end of the first line. They say you need to ride the rails for a while to understand the traveling blues. They're wrong. To understand the traveling blues you need to be locked down somewhere. In a cell. Or in the army. Someplace where you're caged. Someplace where smokestack lightning looks like a faraway beacon of impossible freedom. I lay there with my coat as a pillow and listened to the music in my head. At the end of the third chorus, I fell asleep.

Reacher's entire situation at that moment has the feel of a blues song. He may be an embodiment of freedom, but he finds himself unjustly incarcerated. Sitting in his cell, consoling himself with the blues, he is an emblem of the book's theme of compromised liberty.

Takeaway

- Set-up and pay-off structures are seen throughout the novel. Sometimes, they allow us to enjoy being ahead of the investigators, but sometimes they just create a sense of structure.
- At other times, the investigators are allowed to get ahead of the reader – that's why they're heroes and we're not!
- Different passages in the novel create different impressions of pace or relaxation. There's a suite of tools for controlling these effects.
- Pace is not always about excitement. Sometimes it's about saving time on boring tasks.
- Lee Child's chapters are largely unstructured, although they may end on a cliffhanger (of which there are various types).
- Scenes sometimes have an event dropped into the middle of them that warns of a later occurrence. This provides readers with useful landmarks.

- The romance sub-plot presents a challenge to Reacher's individualistic values.
- The race subplot provides a moral commentary on the main plot.

9. DESCRIPTION AND DIALOGUE

'Can you give me a description of him?'
'Before he got his face shot off?'
- Lee Child, *Killing Floor*

This final chapter is a celebration of the micro-craft in *Killing Floor*: those wordsmithing techniques that should be in the repertoire of every aspiring writer.

Description

If you've read any book about creative writing, or attended any workshop, the chances are you will have been told to describe things by reference to all the senses. What you are less likely to have been told is that brevity is everything in description. Lee Child is the master of giving a couple of telling details that evoke the whole atmosphere of a thing.

For example, in Chapter 2, Reacher describes the exterior of the police headquarters, and one of the things he focuses on is, unexpectedly, the rubber seal around the door. It makes a sucking sound as it opens and closes. It's very difficult to say why that single detail evokes the nature of the police headquarters, but it really does create a creepy impression. Does it suggest that the police are a tense, sealed-off elite? Or does it make the building seem like a creature slowly ingesting the people who enter it? It's difficult to say, but it works, and it depends on a single sense: hearing.

To achieve a really vivid description, focus only on those sensations that seem to evoke the whole nature of a thing. That will mean using some senses and ignoring others. There's a common-sense element to this. After all, it would be ludicrous to describe the smell of a door seal, given that no one goes around sniffing such things. But there's also a poetic element to the process. You have to trust your deep, pre-rational imagination to tell you which sensations are most evocative.

Reacher's description of the prison in Chapter 5 provides an interesting contrast to the spareness of the door description. Here, a number of senses are referred to: smell ('the night exhalation of countless dispirited men'); hearing (the muttering and whimpering of the prisoners); sight (the building's appearance, which is 'like a solid block of masonry'). This multi-sensory description is convincing because it occurs at a moment when Reacher is just lying there taking in his environment. It suggests wandering thoughts. But it's important to note that each sensory perception is still evoked in the minimum of words – a brief, telling detail.

One way that Lee Child enhances the vividness of Reacher's perceptions is through the 'music' of his prose. By that, I mean the rhythm and patterning of his words. For example, in Chapter 1, the words 'heat' and 'steam' are repeated, creating a sense of their oppressiveness. Later, in Chapter 5, the description of the prison seems to drill itself into your consciousness through the repetition of 'cage' and 'wire'. On a slightly larger scale, the description of Reacher's induction into the prison is extremely claustrophobic because it gives a mass of detail about layer after layer of security.

Another truism about description that you find in most books on creative writing is the idea that you must remain firmly within the character's viewpoint. In other words, you must never describe anything that your viewpoint character would not consciously notice. In addition, you must be faithful to the way they would see the world. That is very much the orthodoxy in creative-writing circles. As we saw in the first chapter, Lee Child's writing is generally an exemplary display of character-saturated narration, but there are occasional tiny slip-ups in the things he notices and how he perceives them. I note this only to show how easy it is fall into viewpoint traps – not to detract from Lee Child's abilities. For example, in Chapter 4, we're given a description of a car pulling up outside the police headquarters, and my feeling is that the description reflects the author's British background.

> I saw Baker's patrol car yaw and bounce into the driveway. No flashing lights. It came slowly around the semicircle and eased to a stop. Bounced once on its springs.

Lee Child (real name Jim Grant, born 1952 in Birmingham, England) is famous for having adopted American language and culture to an almost perfect degree in his novels. But here, I think he gives away his Englishness by having Reacher remark on the 'bouncing' movement of the vehicle on its typically soft American suspension. There's a distinct difference between the engineering of European and American cars, and this bouncing movement is something that only a European would consider worth describing.

In Chapter 18, there's another car description that doesn't quite ring true. It's the reference to how a car 'gulped and shot forward.' This time, it's not a European way of looking at the world that interrupts the Reacher viewpoint. Rather, it's the brief intrusion of a literary mindset. The phrase 'gulped and shot forward' has a vivid little personification built into it. It sounds like the product of a writer in his study, not a former military policeman in the thick of the action. This kind of momentary lapse into purple prose is the most common flaw in both amateur and professional writing. In third-person narratives they are much more common because of the slight distance from the viewpoint character.

So far, we've been discussing descriptive passages that are intended purely to create a sense of vividness. But there are many other reasons for providing the reader with description, and *Killing Floor* has examples of several.

Description can be used to lend a sense of authenticity to the fictional world. That's to say, it can make you feel that the narrator really does know what they're talking about. Of course, some environments are more unfamiliar to readers than others, and raise more questions about authenticity as a result. Equally, some environments are more interesting to readers than others, creating a stronger desire for convincing information. The military and police environments that Reacher knows so well are both unfamiliar and interesting to readers. We just gobble up factual details about them, whether those details are humdrum, like the fingerprinting in Chapter 2, or geeky, like the information in Chapter 5 about bullet speeds and noise levels. A few gory details are always thrilling, like the reference to small critters eating the lips and eyes of a body in Chapter 9. This is a good example of how authenticity doesn't necessarily come from large amounts of information. It comes from small, significant details. A barrage of research would, if anything, break the fictional illusion, as the reader would become aware of the author and their research effort. For some people, this is a problem with the novels of Frederick Forsyth, or Patrick O'Brian, to take two prominent examples. However, as the success of those two authors shows, there is a market for literature that barely disguises its research.

The tradecraft used by military characters has an especially large and eager following. In particular, detailed information about the devices and techniques used to kill and maim seems to be a must in certain types of thriller. One problem that authors face is that readers are now incredibly well-versed in this sort of thing. Our everyday vocabulary has been thoroughly colonised by Glocks and Uzis. Lee Child does provide some of that. Each of his novels tends to have a named super weapon, like the Desert Eagle in *Killing Floor*. But he's more of a specialist in describing deadly improvised techniques – approaches to killing that use an everyday item and leave you thinking: Wow I never saw it in that light. For example, in Chapter 18, we read that the best way to dispose of a body is to leave it in the trunk of a car and park it at an airport's long-stay carpark. Genius! If your character can find a lethal use for something that most people have in their home, that has a special thrill. In the ambush at the Hubble residence, Reacher uses a number of household items to devastating effect. Waterproof mascara, skiing gloves and an old hat are repurposed as camouflage, for example.

To make opportunities for this kind of 'tradecraft' description, Lee Child does an interesting thing. He draws attention to the fact that he is addressing people who don't know Reacher's world. For example, when he cuts someone's throat in Chapter 26, he explains in gory detail what that means: 'You don't do it with one elegant swipe.' On the face of it, this might seem to be another flaw in the consistency of the narrator's viewpoint. As we have seen, most creative writing books recommend only describing things that would stand out to the viewpoint character. Cutting throats is something Reacher knows about, so, by the conventional wisdom, we should not be hearing about it. But, I'm afraid that only goes to show there are no real rules in creative writing. It either works or it doesn't. In the case of tradecraft, it clearly works to withdraw momentarily from the action and give a little seminar. In fact, one of the main reasons why people buy Lee Child's books is so that they can be schooled in the arts of life and death by Jack Reacher. That doesn't mean you have permission to hose the reader down with any old information, of course. It has to be information with a proven following. Otherwise it would break the viewpoint and bore everyone rigid.

A word of warning: when you get into describing any sort of detail, you are in danger of committing errors of fact or consistency. As we have seen, Lee Child is not the type of author who overloads us with researched detail, so errors of fact are not usually a problem. He has, however, admitted that Jack Reacher's former rank of Major is inconsistent with the type of military-policing work ascribed to him in other novels. The success of the novels illustrates how unimportant those kinds of facts are to the type of readers Lee Child attracts. The key is to know your market and provide the level of detail they are expecting.

Errors of consistency, by contrast, are a problem in most types of fiction. Lee Child is clearly aware that they have the potential to distract and annoy readers. In the ambush scene discussed earlier, he is careful to justify the presence of gloves and hats in the cupboard of a Georgia family. In my view, he's a little too sensitive about those kinds of issues. Merely looking like you're heading off reader criticisms can ruin the illusion that it's Jack Reacher addressing you. As in the Wizard of Oz, it can only be a disappointment if the curtain's pulled aside and the author's spotted pulling the strings of the characters.

Let's consider another function of description in *Killing Floor*. In Chapter 14, we see Mayor Teale at the police headquarters. We're given a number of details that, together, provide an indirect way of getting to know the guy. For one thing, he's a Cadillac driver – a brand with 'rich-old-guy' associations. Not only that, but Teale's Cadillac is full of showy features, like 'puffy black leather and fake wood.' The man's suit, silver hair, bootlace tie and cane with a silver knob complete the impression that he's an old reactionary. This indirect characterisation through descriptive detail is used by Lee Child in a small number of places. It's reserved for those characters who have a major role, especially on the criminal side of things.

The next type of description in *Killing Floor* could broadly be described as symbolic. In other words, there are some details that aren't about conveying physical appearance, or even hinting at human character, but rather about communicating one of the themes of the novel. This is a huge subject in its own right, but to illustrate my point, I'll discuss just one example: the Desert Eagle.

This awesome weapon is provided to Reacher by Roscoe in Chapter 17. She explains that it belonged to Gray. This is clearly meant to be its most significant characteristic, since Lee Child returns to the subject of Gray's ownership in Chapter 19. At that stage, we also hear about Gray's tragic suicide – a story which will later turn out to be a slanderous concoction. What are we to make of this? Is it just poetic justice that Reacher takes up the dead cop's gun and uses it to kill his slanderers and Joe's murderers? I don't think so. I think the richness of meaning associated with the Desert Eagle goes way beyond that. Importantly, it's an altogether different class of weapon than Roscoe's little revolver. For one thing, it has a rather poetic name. It's also more impressive in its size and stopping power than the standard police .38. We see them together in Chapter 19 and the contrast is apparent.

> Roscoe laid her shiny .38 on the carpet on her side of the bed. I reloaded my giant .44 and laid it on my side.

So, the Desert Eagle seems to represent a different type of authority – one that's quite different from police authority. That's a strange characteristic for a weapon that belonged to a policeman. But there's an explanation for it. The Desert Eagle's profile seems to echo a theme discussed in a previous chapter: the idea that, when all authority is compromised, any decent person in a position of responsibility will throw the rules out of the window.

Towards the end of the novel, almost every descriptive detail is symbolic in some way, by which I mean that it recalls some aspect of theme. The Desert Eagle becomes part of this deepening of symbolic meaning as Reacher uses it to blow away Kliner and (eventually) Picard. That moment is all about the triumph of legitimate authority over illegitimate authority.

The final way description is used in *Killing Floor* actually relates quite closely to this ramping up of the symbolic level. Essentially, descriptive details are used to highlight moments of emotional intensity. The most obvious examples occur in Chapters 15 and 25. In both those places, Reacher describes the breaking of a storm. In the first case, it suggests the release of sexual tension when Roscoe and Reacher finally get it together.

> She was wearing black underwear beneath the uniform. Not very substantial items. We ended up in a frenzy on the bedroom floor. The thunderstorm was finally breaking outside.

In the second instance, a building storm hints at the impending violence as Reacher prepares to ambush the Kliner boy and his kill squad.

> They came for me at twenty minutes past midnight. The rain was still bad and the thunder was still crashing and rolling.

For all those creative writing nerds out there, the use of weather to reflect human emotion is technically known as the 'pathetic fallacy.'

Lee Child also uses non-weather-related details to reflect characters' emotions. There's a particularly moving example in Chapter 20. Molly – who was probably Joe's lover – takes a huge risk by coming to meet with Reacher. But before they can hook up, she's murdered in the most sinister way: she's dragged off into the baggage handling area and cut open. And while that's happening, her slashed suitcase comes wobbling out on the baggage carousel, alone and unclaimed. It's a highly poignant hint at her lonely life and even lonelier death.

Settings

Although certain important settings in *Killing Floor* are described in a fairly vivid (though economical) way, vividness is not a primary concern for Lee Child (or most thriller writers). The settings feel like they are just vivid enough, but not at all deep. To describe them as 'stage sets' would be an exaggeration, but it's not far from the truth. We have no real sense of Margrave as a human ecosystem, and we only have the barest outline of its geography and appearance.

All of us have a mental database of TV and movie imagery, especially when it comes to those familiar thriller settings: the police headquarters, the prison, the motel room, the villain's industrial unit, etc. Writers can appeal to this database with a very few words. As a descriptive technique, it has the advantage of being highly economical, which puts the minimum number of obstacles in the way of slick storytelling. Slick storytelling is, after all, what thrillers are all about.

But what the settings of *Killing Floor* lack in descriptive depth, they make up for in depth of meaning. Several times in this book, I've had cause to use the word 'allegory', and it's appropriate here too, as a way of looking at Lee Child's description of locations. To some extent, the sense of place in a Jack Reacher novel is rather like the sense of place in a medieval poem. After reading *Gawain and the Green Knight*, for example, you have no idea at all what Camelot looks like, but you certainly know what it stands for: nobility, order and civilisation.

It's the same with Margrave. The author only describes those features of the town that tell us what it stands for in thematic terms. As Reacher is walking with Roscoe to the Hubble residence in Chapter 10, we hear about how isolated from one another the houses are. This is more than just a sociological observation, it's a metaphor for social fragmentation in a prosperous society. The metaphor reveals its meaning in a slow but satisfying fashion. The eerie neatness of Margrave is observed several times during Reacher's perambulations – the first time is in Chapter 9, while he's waiting to meet up with Roscoe. In Chapter 16, during a discussion at the barber's shop, we discover that money is being pumped into all the town's businesses. That's the first unfolding of the metaphor. Then, in Chapter 22, Reacher realises that 'The whole town was in it. The whole place was bought and paid for.' That's the final release of meaning. Margrave stands revealed as an emblem for the hollowness at the heart of a society structured around money.

There's a literary term for this kind of symbolic place. We call it a 'locus' (plural 'loci'). The two other loci that are most noticeable in *Killing Floor* are the barber's shop and the police headquarters.

The barber's premises are particularly saturated with symbolic detail. For example, it's a repository of truth in several senses. Firstly, it's the location of Gray's lost case notes that implicate Kliner. Secondly, it's the home of a woman who remembers how Blind Blake died. This 'truth beacon' meaning of the barber shop is reinforced when Reacher and Hubble arrive in town, intent on rescuing Charlie and Roscoe. The only light on in Margrave at that time is the light at the barber's shop.

The police headquarters is less developed as a locus of thematic meaning, but it does have a certain amount of symbolic resonance. Before their visit to the barber's shop, en route to Kliner's warehouse, Reacher and Hubble rescue Finlay. Significantly, they rescue him from his own police headquarters, trashing it comprehensively. It's a perfect distillation of that theme I've been harping on about: when the authorities are totally corrupt, the only decent expression of authority is to resist them.

There is another reason for the relative flatness of the description of Margrave. It's to do with the conventions of crime fiction. If I say that Lee Child's novels are similar to those of Agatha Christie in at least one respect, please try not to laugh. Even if you've never read one of Miss Christie's legendary novels, I'm sure you're aware that they often revolve around a single village or country house. The detective moves from area to area within that confined setting, learning more about the case at each stop. Although it's not an exact parallel, the way Reacher moves around the confined world of Margrave – specifically in Chapter 9 – is reminiscent of that familiar structure. At each stop – the barber's, the convenience store and the pathologist's office – he learns more about the criminality affecting the world of the novel.

Dialogue

Dialogue performs some of the same functions as description in *Killing Floor*. Namely, it evokes character and creates a feeling of authenticity. For example, in Chapter 6, the accent of a Southern black man in prison is rendered using little more than a single characteristic phrase.

> 'I've been in this joint since God's dog was a puppy, yes sir. Since Adam was a young boy. But here's something I ain't never seen. No sir, not in all those years.'

The words 'yes sir' (and 'no sir'), and perhaps a distinctive flavour to the imagery, are enough to tell us about this guy's racial background, Southern origins and state of mind (a little batty).

It's good to err on the side of subtlety when it comes to suggesting accents and character traits through speech. It can sound patronising and hold the reader up by forcing them to decipher your non-standard spellings. The conversation between Reacher and Kelstein in Chapter 25 is a tour de force of ultra-subtle phrasing changes and vocabulary choices. Consider the phrase 'But you remain skeptical?' It's clearly the utterance of an intelligent man used to phrasing ideas in formal language. He could have said 'But you don't believe them?' Consider also the phrase 'Your brother was Mr. Joe Reacher?' The unnecessary use of 'Mr.' and the inverted sentence order make this sound unmistakably like a non-native speaker of English.

These language effects are often backed up by brief descriptions of gestures. To my eye, 'Kelstein cupped his hands like a man holding an empty vessel' suggests that the professor has Central-European Jewish origins.

Gestures are important for conveying psychological as well as sociological information. During his prison conversation with Reacher, Hubble is said to be 'writhing around like my questions were tearing him up.' Similarly, when Finlay is interviewing Reacher, the cop's body language is described over and over again, illustrating the changing balance of power in the conversation. Reacher's in-text interpretations of Finlay's gestures further contribute to the feeling that he's holding the whip.

He sat there, breathing hard. In trouble.
…
Finlay opened his mouth. And closed it. He needed to save some face. Badly.
…
Finlay gazed at me. Drummed his fingers on the desk. Kept quiet.
…
He looked at me. A bit rueful. Like he'd forgotten I was there.
…
He glared at me briefly. Turned back to Baker.
…
He glared at me again and left the room. Banged the heavy door.

But the very best dialogue and gesture descriptions don't reveal character and motivation in an open and obvious way. It's a more powerful effect if a character's interior life remains hidden, while their words or actions suggest an untrue picture. It's a great skill to write dialogue that jars with the reader's instincts and so reveals itself as false. In Chapter 14, Reacher encounters Mayor Teale at the police precinct.

> 'I understood you were just passing through,' he said. 'We have no hotel here in Margrave and I imagined you would find no opportunity to stay.'
> 'I'm staying,' I said. 'I received a generous offer of hospitality. I understand that's what the South is famous for, right? Hospitality?'
> He beamed at me and grasped his embroidered lapel.
> 'Oh, undoubtedly that's true, sir,' he said. 'The South as a whole, and Georgia in particular, is indeed famous for the warmth of its welcome. However, as you know, just at the present time, we find ourselves in a most awkward predicament. In the circumstances, a motel in Atlanta or Macon would really suit you much better.

Ostensibly, Mayor Teale is being solicitous about Reacher's welfare, while Reacher is innocently stating his intention to stick around. But of course, we know the subtext. Teale wants Reacher gone and Reacher knows that Teale is a vicious old reactionary.

Revealing character and motivation is by no means the only purpose of dialogue. In fact, it has five essential functions:

- Moving the plot along
- Summarising where we have got to in the plot
- Exposition of information the reader needs to know
- Dramatising conflict
- Revealing character and motivation

Placing too much emphasis on just one of these functions of dialogue would come across as tedious and fake. But, like all good novels, *Killing Floor* takes advantage of each function as needed.

Lee Child also knows exactly when to use dialogue and when to use action. For the whole of the first chapter, there's practically no dialogue, apart from screamed commands from the police as they arrest Reacher. Instead, we're given Reacher's internal commentary about the events going on around him. In a situation when he could have seemed weak and at a disadvantage, he ends up seeming in control because he withholds himself from open conflict or verbal engagement. In fact, because we are located securely behind Reacher's eyes and in his thoughts, he seems more real than the relatively impersonal police officers.

In Chapter 2, by contrast, Lee Child gives us a feast of dialogue after the famine of Chapter 1. This is not only desirable because the plot demands it, but also because a change of texture refreshes the reader.

Takeaway

- Lee Child uses all the senses in descriptions, but always the right sense in the right place.
- He also uses the rhythm of sentences to enhance descriptions.
- *Killing Floor* consistently reflects the viewpoint character's personality in descriptions. But acknowledging the presence of an audience and their information needs is NOT considered taboo.
- Technical detail adds authenticity to descriptions of militaria and violence in the novel, but it's used sparingly. Lee Child knows his readers' preferences.
- We also see description used in the following ways.
  - o Characterisation of an individual's personality or social profile.
  - o Symbolically evoking some aspect of the novel's theme.
  - o Setting the emotional level.
- Descriptions of places are relatively flat in *Killing Floor*, because they are intended
  - o to act as symbolic loci;
  - o to provide a stylised backdrop to investigative activity.
- Gesture is frequently used to help dialogue convey psychological and sociological information.

- There are a number of speeches in which characters say something other than what they really feel. The author makes the truth available to the reader, usually by setting it up in the preceding action.
- Lee Child uses dialogue to achieve various different effects. Each use of dialogue is in balance with the others. Variety is everything.

CONCLUSION

Congratulations on reaching the end of the book. What now?

If you haven't signed up for my email list to get the accompanying exercises, I encourage you to do so. See the special offer at the end of the book for details. Working through those targeted activities is the best way to extract maximum value from this book. They will help you to complete much of the preparation for writing a great thriller.

I would also encourage you to read the many other Jack Reacher novels by Lee Child. As you do so, you'll probably notice quite a few of the structures and stylistic gestures that I've described here. In fact, analysing the similarities and differences will help you internalise the lessons drawn from *Killing Floor.*

Not all of what I've pointed out in Lee Child's work will make sense to you, but that's OK. It shows you're becoming your own kind of writer. The key is to practise, work out what you want to keep, and leave the rest behind – like Reacher himself.

> I looked out at the southeast corner of Alabama. Opened Roscoe's envelope. It was the photograph of Joe. She'd taken it from Molly Beth's valise. Taken it out of the frame. Trimmed it with scissors to fit my pocket. On the back she had written her telephone number. But I didn't need that. I had already committed it to memory.

SPECIAL OFFER

A comprehensive set of exercises accompanies *Write Like Lee Child*. The 35-page workbook will walk you through the process of planning a novel in the style of Lee Child, and help you practise thriller-writing techniques.

To receive the writing exercises for FREE, all you have to do is sign up for my *Popular Fiction Masterclass* email newsletter. Go to the Web address below, then follow the on-screen instructions.

http://popularfictionmasterclass.com/106-2/

THANK YOU FOR CHOOSING THIS BOOK

If you enjoyed reading it and working through the exercises, I'd be delighted if you could leave a review on Amazon. Positive feedback from readers helps me a great deal and it's always great to hear what like-minded people think of my work. Go to the Web address below, then click on the image of this book. You'll be taken to the relevant Amazon page.

http://popularfictionmasterclass.com/about/

It would also be great to see you on my Facebook page. That's where we continue the discussion of subjects raised in the *Popular Fiction Masterclass* series of books.

https://www.facebook.com/pfmasterclass/

To browse other titles in this series, please go to the following Web address.

http://popularfictionmasterclass.com/about/

Printed in Great Britain
by Amazon

26827858R00098